RELEASE willingly
PURPOSEFULLY
to God

RELEASE willingly PURPOSEFULLY to God

AWAKEN THE SPIRIT WITHIN and quiet the tyrannical mind

L. PATRICK KASTNER

MILL CITY PRESS

Mill City Press, Inc.
2301 Lucien Way #415
Maitland, FL 32751
407.339.4217
www.millcitypress.net

© 2018 by L. Patrick Kastner

Scripture quotations taken from:

the English Standard Version (ESV). Copyright © 2001 by Crossway, a publishing ministry of Good News Publishers. Used by permission. All rights reserved.

the King James Version (KJV) – *public domain.*

the Holy Bible, New International Version (NIV). Copyright © 1973, 1978, 1984, 2011 by Biblica, Inc.™. Used by permission. All rights reserved.

the Holy Bible, New Living Translation (NLT). Copyright ©1996, 2004, 2007 by Tyndale House Foundation. Used by permission of Tyndale House Publishers, Inc.

Printed in the United States of America

ISBN-13: 978-1-54563-814-9

This book is dedicated to my best friend, God, who has watched over and guided me my entire life. God has been ever present and active in the creative thoughts and ideas that have become a part of this book. God has counseled me and watched over me, instructed, taught, and kept His eyes upon me. It is by God's grace that I have been blessed to publish this book.

I also dedicate this book to David R (Ross) Young-Wolf, 1951–2017. A Native American, (GWY) full-blooded Cherokee, and Master Wood Carver, whose words "Finish that book and get it published" echo in my mind in memory of the friendship and in-depth, although brief, discussions we shared about life and spirituality. David, RIP

Eagle carved and signed by David

TABLE OF CONTENTS

AUTHOR'S NOTE

As a point of clarification, it is important to note that while many of the essays herein make reference to the "Holy Spirit Within", they are in no way intended to be in conflict with Christian teachings.

It is often mentioned and referred to by clergy and others that in order to be saved, one must be reborn again in Christ Jesus. This is what the references in the essays "Awakening the Holy Spirit Within" pertain to.

While the implication is that The Holy Spirit of God becomes a part one one's life when the person "becomes born again", the presumption put forth throughout the essays is that the Holy Spirit of God, the Spark, is in every individual from the time of conception.

It is one's individualism, which is represented in the time, event, place, or circumstance wherein that spark ignites the acceptance and recognition of the role God plays and is a part of their life.

It is the purpose of the examples and analogies presented here to cause the reader to pause and recognize how their life is fulfilled through "The Awakening of the Holy Spirit of God Within".

This book is dedicated to God, who has not only inspired me in writing these essays and words of Inspiration, but who has watched over me and guided me throughout my life, even when I was undeserving and unworthy of His love.

May God's Light Shine upon you, His Love enfold you and His Blessings enrich your life as you reflect upon what is presented here.

AWAKEN THE POWER OF THE "INDWELLING SPIRIT"

"so that you may abound in hope by the power of the Holy Spirit"

Romans 15:13 (NIV)

**In all things see, the presence of God,
the serendipity of life.**

Recognize and affirm God's many blessings

because

fulfillment comes through the awareness

of

the Spirit of God within.

PREFACE
(The Pilot Light—The Spark)

The most significant discovery on this earth that man has made other than that of exploring the earth itself is fire. The benefits of fire are unlimited. Fire is a source of light and heat, a means by which to light the way, a medium used in the process of preparing and preserving food, and an unending resource used in manufacturing and industry.

The means of igniting a fire are many: from the use of a flintstone to make a spark, a stick rubbed on a rock, or the magnified sun to concentrate heat to ignite tinder, man has found and used many sources to ignite a substance that results in producing fire. In the twentieth century, a source of sparks has made possible the combustion engine that powers our vehicles, pilot lights that have become the convenient source of igniting a flame to heat water, homes, and entire buildings. In more recent times the pilot light has been replaced with igniters and glow plugs, which, when utilized, provide a spark to combustible liquids in many applications and types of appliances. While the principle is basically similar in each situation—spark (ignition), combustion (flame), and fire (heat)—the results are a functional resource that provide benefits to mankind. Without them there wouldn't be huge furnaces that produce steel or the source that ignites the rockets that propel man into outer space.

In like manner, God has instilled in every person a basic source with which to enkindle the glowing torch within. That source is much like the pilot light or igniter on an appliance that operates to ignite a type of combustible-like gas. This basic source is determined as a child develops. It is the source within that the child will have that through life will ignite a type of combustion and "Awaken the Power of the Indwelling Spirit Within." As a child develops, the environment in which the child is exposed, even before birth, will have a bearing on what will spark the burning flame within. Every single person, at the moment they are conceived, is instilled with the Holy Spirit, the flame of God within. In an Exhilarating Climactic Moment Man and Woman May Have Conceived a Child. However, In That Loving Purposeful

Moment, God Created a Child with an Indwelling Spirit. As a person grows from infancy, to childhood, into their youthful years, and to adulthood, the ever-glowing pilot light, the Flame of God within, is able to ignite the Spirit of God, resulting in the blessings of love, peace, and fulfillment.

For some, with parents living lives according to God's plan, the source within the child that is able to spark the burning flame within, the Holy Spirit, will be activated with every loving experience. As the child is exposed to the lifestyle, instruction, and guidance of the parents and others, that spark will become an ever-burning flame that generates the blessings of love, peace, and fulfillment through. "Awakening the Power of the Holy Spirit Within" throughout their life.

For some, the lifestyle, instruction, and guidance in the early years of their life may snuff out any flame, leaving the child from infancy, to childhood, into their youthful years, and perhaps even to adulthood, with nothing more than the basic source with which to enkindle the glowing torch. Then something, a person, circumstance, a publication, will push that button on the igniter, and suddenly a spark lights that flame, changing their life by "Awakening the Power of the Holy Spirit Within" and filling their life with the blessings of love, peace, and fulfillment.

For others, life's circumstances may deny them the gift of ever having the resources instilled by God to create a spark to ignite the flame of the "Awakened Power of the Holy Spirit Within." Their tyrannical mind or that of others may try to douse—extinguish—and quench any source of a spark or flame in their lives.

It is to these, and to those who have not yet had those resources, provided by God, activated in their lives that this book is dedicated. If one word, one phrase, one sentence, paragraph, or analogy brings the resources God has placed there to ignite that flame and "Awaken the Power of the Holy Spirit Within," praise God for having been Present and Active in the Creative Thoughts and Ideas presented here.

GOD IN SPIRIT

A Spirit That Moves About Quietly, Gently, Ever Present, All Knowing, Touching Lovingly.

A Spirit That's Establishing, Fulfilling, Inspiring, Motivating, Making Paths Where There Appear to Be None and Closing Doors That Appear to Lead to Danger.

A Spirit That Is Embracing, Enfolding, Teaching, Counseling, and Showing the Way.

A Spirit That Is the Inspiration Behind Every Idea and the Facilitator of Every Endeavor.

A Spirit That Is the Light in the Darkness, Calm in the Midst of a Storm, Courage in the Face of Trials, Strength Where There Is Weakness, Healing and Comfort Where There Is Pain, Joy in the Event of Sorrow, Laughter to Lighten a Heavy Heart.

A Spirit That Paints on the Canvas We Call Sky, the Craftsman That Creates Every Aspect of Nature and the Birther of Every Living Creature and the Very Heart and Soul of Every Human Being.

Awaken the Holy Spirit Within Each One of Us, Lord, That We Might Answer Your Call by Releasing Ourselves to You So That We Might Be Your Instruments of Love and Peace. Excite Each of Us in Knowing That Your Presence Is Eternal, Your Love Is Unyielding, and Your Supernatural Wisdom Is Guiding Us to Our Highest Good.

O' Mighty God, Praise You. Be It Not Our Cry but Our Song That Delights You. May Our Heart Embrace You, Our Mind Be Focused upon You, and May Our Actions Please You. Amen.

RELEASE
VS.
SURRENDER

Reference is often made by religious orators that it is important, even necessary, to **surrender** oneself to God to be "saved."

Would it not be more appropriate to **release** oneself to God that He might guide a person in fulfilling one's purpose in life?

Surrendering is associated with giving up, giving in, admitting defeat, acknowledging weakness or the inability to overcome.

Releasing, associating with turning over, letting go, giving freely, indicates having control and the willingness to relinquish, which denotes intent, commitment, strength.

When a person surrenders they are suggesting an inability to stand with confidence, or to move decisively. In the context of one's relationship with God, this person is saying, "I'm not worthy, nor do I pose the qualities or ability to be the person You want me to be."

However, when one releases themselves to God, they are proposing that they are blessed and well able, through the gifts they have been given by God, to follow His direction in fulfilling His plan for their life. By releasing one's heart, mind, soul, and entire being to God, one is saying they are strong, committed, prepared, and completely willing to be the embodiment of God through which God is able to communicate with them and with others through them.

Jesus Christ did not surrender Himself. He released Himself to God that God might use Him to teach, demonstrate, show by example, and, yes, even work miracles in the lives of others.

Is it that mankind should be worried about being "saved" by striving to do what the "opinion of man" suggests is necessary? Or is it not more likely that by releasing one's soul, heart, mind, and entire being to God that they will serve God, by which His light will shine brightly upon them, guiding them in fulfilling His purpose for their life on earth.

There is something exhilarating about giving freely, without conditions, reservations, or expectations. Giving the best of what a person has, something valued, an important part of themselves. Giving something that works, isn't broken or impaired, and is of high quality, meaningful, and significant.

On the other hand, to surrender is to approach with cup in hand, humbly as though unworthy. Surrendering denotes the likelihood of reluctance, the lack of willingness as though obligatory. Surrendering tends to always have conditions, expectations, often begrudgingly. Often surrendering is accompanied with rationalizations such as: insignificant, meaningless of little use, didn't need it anyway. It's like giving one's gallbladder, considered a bodily part of no purpose or need, rather than one's heart, which is the most significant part of the human body.

To release one's heart to God is to offer something vital, genuine, meaningful, and steadfast.

RESTORATION

While
People delight in restoring things:
cars, houses, tractors, old buildings, and a number of aged and otherwise abandoned things.
God delights in Restoring People.

A person can take a vintage car, spend hours working on it, spend large amounts of money, and restore it to its original condition. It need not necessarily be an old car in the number of years it's been around. However, it may have been driven hard, dented and abused, battered by other vehicles, and perhaps even abandoned. Certainly, a far and poor example of what it once was.

The restorer may start by removing every worn, damaged, and corroded part, and strip the car down to its basic frame; then part by part clean, repair, remanufacture, and reassemble every aspect of the car. As a result, when all is done everything will be working and looking like when it was new. The motor will purr without missing a beat. The drive train will perform in unison with the motor to provide smooth acceleration and travel. The interior will look and smell of newness, unblemished as it once had been when first put into service. The exterior, without a scratch or dent, will glisten with the brightness and shine of a new car. Above all, the restorer will pamper, wash, polish, and take every precaution to keep this renewed gem functioning and looking excellent and in perfect condition. Thereby reflecting in the care, attention, pride, joy, and interest the restorer has in protecting this handiwork.

So Too:

God is able, in like manner, to take a person, who need not necessarily be old in the number of years they have been around and spend great resources in their restoration. Perhaps they have been driven hard during their life and become damaged; physically, mentally, and spiritually. It could be that they have been battered, bruised, taken advantage of by others, and perhaps even abandoned by society. Certainly, a far and poor example of what God created them to be.

God may start by removing every worn, damaged, and used part of their life and strip the person down to the bare basics. Then step by step through the awakening of the Spirit of God within, with love, guidance, and possible intervention, repair and reassemble every aspect of that person. As a result, when all is done everything will be renewed. Spiritually the person will experience their oneness with God. Their physical makeup will function without missing a beat. Their drive and ambition will allow them to perform in unison with God's plan for their life. Their attitude will shine forth with a newness and look unblemished as it had been when they were first brought into this world. Their physique, though scratched and scarred, will glow with the brightness and shine of God's love. Above all, God will bless, pamper, and take every precaution to keep this renewed soul functioning and remaining excellent. Thereby reflecting upon the love, care, attention, pride, joy, and interest that God has in protecting His handiwork.

SUMMARY

A person may consider themselves forgotten, lost, and unappreciated, which could be like what had happened to the old car. They may have succumbed to the pressures, doubts, and frustrations of life, and turned to material reward or an abusive habit. However, there is one interested in their restoration, and that one is God. God will, and is able to, do anything to bless, pamper, and take every step and precaution to keep this renewed soul functioning according to the plan God has for their life.

The old car is helpless on its own to go and turn to the restorer for help. Whereas, man need only ask, and the restorer, God, will make His presence known in the individual's life and begin the restoration process to a renewed life of love, peace, joy, and fulfillment.

"For you, O Lord, are good and forgiving, abounding in
steadfast love to all who call upon you."
Psalm 86:5 (ESV)

MEDITATION MADE EASY

Generally, it's considered that meditation is beneficial to those who practice it. For many, if not most, meditating is for one reason or another difficult or seemingly impossible. The busy, complicated, troubled lives filled with concerns, worries, difficulties, interruptions, emergencies, etc., keep people from committing themselves to regular or even infrequent periods of meditation. Some people who make valiant attempts to meditate, while attempting to avoid the distractions and make their best effort, wonder if they have truly achieved a true state of meditation and if they have experienced the benefits meditation is espoused to provide. There are a number of people who would spend a few minutes meditating if they could truly experience its benefits and realize its impact on their daily lives.

There is a way. Some may consider it unconventional. No matter, if it works, that is what is important. The fact is, there is one thing that every person meditates on consciously and even subconsciously, and that is their appearance. In fact, the way one views their appearance influences a number of ways they spend their time, resources, and energy. Stop and think about how much time is spent doing the things that allow one to feel good about oneself just in their grooming, their bodily cleanliness and aroma, their hair and more. Then there are the things one purchases for hygiene, physical appearance, health products and pills, clothes and jewelry, health foods, an unending list. Then there is the effort in dieting, working out, even reading books on health. Yes, people certainly meditate on how they appear to themselves in their mind's eye, in a mirror, and, probably most of all, in the perceived view that they believe others have of them. Yes, people meditate! How often does it result in negative and self-defeating consequences though? Using this same basis for meditation it is possible the result will be just the opposite however.

Start by setting aside just a few minutes. It can be anytime, anyplace, and can probably even be in a surrounding where there is noise and disruption. Remember, though, you're thinking (meditating) about yourself, your appearance, how others see you. One can do that anywhere and often does.

Now visualize yourself as a vessel. Be honest with yourself. Do you see yourself as a plain vase without color or special shape? Perhaps a very fancy vase with many beautiful colors and attractively shaped. You may see many jewels adorning your vase. The vase may be short and fat, tall and slender, and of any color. Maybe it's not even a vase. You could look at yourself as an unattractive pot, some sort of pan, even an old rusty pail. Frankly, it doesn't really matter as long as you are honest with yourself and admitting to yourself how you actually see yourself. It's only your impression of yourself that matters.

Have a clear picture of how you see your outward appearance physically (as the container), then take note of how you feel about yourself internally. Are you stuffing a huge combination of "things" within? They may include anxiety, nervousness, fear, disappointment, heartbreak, greed, joyously, arrogance, revengefulness, even hatred. Looking at your container, visualize starting one by one and scooping those things out. Yes, even the good things. Get everything out of your container. Empty it completely. Scrape the sides of scum, the bottom of all the sediment. Get the rust out, everything. Turn it upside down and shake everything out. Visualize a completely empty, sparkling clean container. It doesn't matter what the outside is or looks like. The important thing is that in your mind's eye the inside is free and clear of absolutely everything,

Now, visualize God beginning to refill your container. God will likely start with peace and serenity, followed by a measure of love mixed in with a little joy. Can you see it starting to flow into your container? See it mixing all together as it begins to fill. Mix in a little self-worth, confidence, courage, wholeness, healing, open-mindedness, acceptance, and visualize God filling the container to the brim.

Then visualize it not stopping there. See buds springing forth from the container and growing and blossoming into a beautiful bouquet of flowers. A bouquet of colorful, full, assorted flowers filling and even overflowing the sides of the container. Concentrate on those flowers and allow their beauty to make an indelible impression in your mind's eye. Visualize your favorite flowers, those you consider the most beautiful. See in your mind's eye a vast variety that blend into the most astounding, diverse, and beautiful bouquet you have ever seen or can imagine. Now, do you even see the container?

Does the container in any way diminish the beauty of the flowers? It's the flowers—that's what God sees. In fact, that's what other people see and influences the way they respond to you.

Your own perception of yourself may even change. As you concentrate on the flowers in your container, visualize the beautiful full red roses and the love and friendships they may represent. Consider the strong, sturdy, green, supporting stems as confidence, self-assurance, and steadfastness. There may be a bright yellow canary perched somewhere on top, indicating patience and understanding. You may even visualize a big bright sunflower rising above it all aglow with happiness, joy, and laughter. Then you may notice the pure white orchid and experience the health and wholeness it may represent in your life.

Yes, life is real. In time, the vision may become dull and faded. All those worldly things will still be bombarding you. However, for one brief moment, everything about you was beautiful. You weren't victimized and held back or limited by the past. You were deemed worthy of God's love and, most importantly, affirmed that you are special, beautiful, and full of the blessings of God's Holy Spirit.

THE BRAIN KNOWS THE RULES.
THE MIND PLAYS THE GAME.

In our brain, over time, we have stored the knowledge of consequences. We know and understand what this or that action will lead to or likely result in.

It's the mind that rationalizes if those consequences are justified. Whether good or bad, wrong, harmful, greedy, or selfish, according to the knowledge we've stored in the brain, the mind is what leads us to action.

READY, SET, GO

In a race of most types, it's standard procedure to cover all aspects necessary to be successful in order to finish as a winner. A competitor goes to great lengths to make themselves ready for the challenge. After dedicated and comprehensive training, testing, and trial attempts, they, their trainer, or mentor determine their "Ready" status and they are "Set" to "Go" and enter the competition. They have met all the requirements, made all the preparations, and acquired everything necessary to begin the challenge.

Life doesn't necessarily work that way however. At least it's not usually the way God interacts in our lives. God does make provision to give us everything we need to fulfill His plan for our lives. Generally, however, for certain challenges in our lives, we may not see or think we have everything we need. All we may be given is just the basics, the thing or things we need to get started; the idea, the motivation, the desire, etc. It is our faith and belief in God and His perfect plan for our lives that moves us to take that first step while not knowing how everything will unfold, or how we'll meet the challenges presented along the way.

With God's plan we don't need dedicated and comprehensive training, testing, or trial attempts to meet all the requirements, make all the preparations, and acquire everything necessary to begin the challenge. Nor do we need a road map, or a guided tour format to follow. That structured agenda, with little or no flexibility, is great for traveling in an unfamiliar area in one's own country or abroad. However, God's plan is one where we are able to experience encounters we otherwise would never have the opportunity to be a part of. While sometimes frightening and challenging, the rewards may be phenomenal.

With God, being "Ready, Set, Go" means, okay God I believe in Your plan for my life. It means I have faith in your providing everything necessary, even when I may not have everything I think I'll need, or even know how or when I will have what it will take. It means taking that first step by doing what it is, that you know what it is that you are able to do. Then having trust and faith that as your trainer or mentor, God, will direct your every step. It means God knows the path that you need to take to achieve His goal for this challenge in your life and for that matter, the overall direction He has set out for your life to follow.

"Ready, Set, Go"? We may be uncertain, but God has everything in order and arranged for. It is for us to have faith, believe in God and in ourselves, and then "GO."

CIRCLING RIPPLE

While beside the water of a lake watching the still waters, the sudden glimpse of a fish coming to the surface to snatch a bug may catch your eye. Seldom do you ever actually see the fish. All you see is the "circling ripple" the fish caused rising to the surface and returning to the depths from which it came. Once seeing this, one is tempted to watch diligently for another fish to emerge for its snack on the surface. Seldom though is there another, and certainly never in the same area or spot.

Many times, God sends little blessings our way in a similar manner, and we hardly even notice. That is, until we recognize the effect it may have had upon us. One little gesture or another makes its way towards us and gives us a warm appreciated feeling. The person that waited and waved for us to enter into heavy traffic. The clerk who made certain that we had everything we had purchased. The greeting we received upon entering a building or the time someone held the door for us. The person who motioned for us to leave a room ahead of them. The ones who said thank you or excuse me. You probably never gave it a thought at the time, but those are the "Circling Ripples" of little blessings with which God pleasures us.

God also blesses us with opportunities to create "Circling Ripples" ourselves. When we favor others by being kind, giving complements, showing respect, offering words of praise and support, we have taken advantage of those opportunities. Many times, just a pleasant smile, a joyful attitude, or a simple nod acknowledging another will make another's day a little brighter. They may even pass the gesture on to someone else, who passes it on to another and another. You see, that ripple you saw the fish make wasn't just one ring in the water, it is one ripple that caused another and another, thus creating the "Circling Ripple".

Get out there and make some "Circling Ripples". Who knows, you may just create a tidal wave of blessings in the lives of many others. For some, what may have been a little blessing for others may just turn out to be a huge blessing that is a life-changing experience. Never underestimate a "Circling Ripple", the little blessing sent our way through another by God, or the one we pass on!

THE FREIGHT TRAIN OF LIFE

The freight train of life consists of a long string of cars of all different types being pulled along by a mighty engine. The engine is God, and each car is carrying a load of issues. However, God is able to pull the cars, no matter how heavily loaded, as long as they remain attached to one another and cling to the engine.

There are cars like the flatcar, fully exposed, with little or no load to be pulled along on the tracks of life. Then there is the heavily laden tightly sealed boxcar loaded with all kinds of junk, closed up tightly, careful so as not to reveal to anyone what is inside. Another, a kind of rickety old car all banged up with rusty stiff wheels making it difficult to move, yet staying on track, clinging to the car ahead, trusting and having faith that the engine, God, will get it to its final destination, God's heavenly train yard.

There are cars like the open gondola, carrying a heavy load, yet one that is open for all to see, one loaded with good things, good deeds. There is the type of car that is neat and clean, well-greased, one which glides along the rails of life with little effort. Then there are those somewhere in between, cars that are clean, brightly colored, well lubricated, carrying a load of good stuff with doors open to everyone so that what is inside can been seen.

There are also cars like the tank car laden with toxic liquids, closed tightly and unexposed. Or a large chemical car, empty, yet carrying the residue of what it once had contained, also closed tightly so no one would ever know what had been inside. Regardless, each of these cars continue to rely on the Engine to pull them through.

These cars, as they pass by on the rail of life, are unlike the cars that have gotten off on the side track, some even completely derailed. Cars that apparently attempted to make it on their own only to find that without the powerful Engine they weren't going to get very far. Cars that have become laden down with issues, banged up and battered, rusty, stiff, and unlubricated, barely able to move even by the most powerful engine.

Yet for these, the side track they are on is still connected to the mainline. With the right help they can still get back onto the main line and be reattached to the mighty Engine to be pulled to their Godly destination.

Sadly, there are those that are far removed from any track, much less a side track connected to the main line. For those cars, so broken up, so buried with issues that they can hardly be distinguished for what they once may have been, there is despair and grieving. The only hope for these cars is for the Mighty Restorer to somehow be beckoned to reach out to make them whole again, enable them to stay on track, carry their load, and one day perhaps even get back onto the main line.

A person may sometimes feel like the caboose, bringing up the rear. Maybe a little more colorful, in spite of all the scrapes and dents, and unlike most ahead of them on this train of life, not carrying much of a load. So, praise God that although at the rear of the train, the powerful Engine, God, is still up ahead pulling you and all the other cars along. Thank God, your faith is strong, and like a tightly gripping coupler, it keeps you connected and on the main line. Even though, particularly being at the very end, with the attractions along the way, it's so tempting at times to want to loosen your grip and slip off on one of those side tracks.

Better that you should be a car well up in the middle of the train, pulling along others who cling to you, trusting that you will not lose your grip and connection to God, the mighty Engine.

THE BIGGEST BLESSING

The most important and biggest blessing a person has in their life is the
recognition and awareness
of the presence of and proactive role that God plays in their life.

From the small insignificant things that occur, to the unlikely and seemingly miraculous events, that play a significant role in a person's life. More often than not, we take things for granted and seldom recognize the connection between certain events where God, in fact, has made His presence apparent. Situations where God played a proactive role in our lives and "Made Things Happen."

There are times and circumstances when we don't make the connection until well after the fact. It is then that we look back with amazement and ask,

"How did that happen?" or
"Wow, now I Get it."

FAILURE

In the eyes and the opinion of man, there is such a thing as failure. In the eyes of God there is no such thing. Even in the eyes and opinion of man, failure is a matter of one's perspective. In one sense it represents defeat and a step backwards, yet in another it represents the opportunity to make a positive move forward and make progress. It's not what others think or judge one by, or what their opinion may be, it's all about how a person perceives a situation. It's how one reacts and responds to how God is working in their life.

When a person is faced with a situation that isn't turning out the way in which they had planned or expected, they have a choice to make. They can be frozen in their tracks, feel defeated, rejected, and allow others to look down upon them and make them feel inferior and a failure. Or, they can look at it as a time for reassessment, reevaluation, readjustment, during which much is learned and therefore accomplished and gained. Rather than the situation being defeating, it can be challenging and embolden a growing, improving experience where one strives for excellence. Stop looking for excuses; rather, seek answers!

God sees each person as an opportunist. A person filled with a future of growth, achievement, and fulfillment. It is difficult enough to overcome the obstacles and negativity in life and what a person faces from the naysayer's. Why be your own worst enemy? Don't add to a difficult situation or contribute to it with your own negative attitude. Negativity tends to shut a person down. Think and act positively, break through the barrier of doubt, it's beautiful and rewarding on the other side.

Free of the opinions of man, releasing one's self to God, one acknowledges "I AM" allowed to be the person God called me to be. What is meant for evil, God will turn it around and use it to His advantage. When life threatens, challenges, disrupts, puts down, or goes against a person, with the help of God it can be turned around and used to their advantage.

THE GIFT

When a baby is born it's not uncommon for the father to give the mother some sort of special gift. There are times that the parents of the mother or father, or even close relatives, will give the happy couple a special gift. These are gestures that generally are greatly appreciated. There is a very special gift that is seldom acknowledged, if ever, which is always given to the newborn child. It's given by the most important one in the child's life and the one who would, or should, play the most significant role in the child's entire span of life. The gracious gift giver, God! The Gift, The Holy Spirit!

Every person, at birth, is instilled with the gift of the Holy Spirit. Sadly, for many the gift will never be appreciated, much less, even acknowledged. For others, the gift will become an integral part of their life. Through parental love and by example the child will experience the grace of God as it influences the pattern their life will follow. As the child grows older, through "The Gift" they will begin to develop individualistic characteristics that reflect the Spirit of God within. As adults, their life will be fulfilling as they maintain that personal relationship and connection with God through the Awakened Spirit Within.

For those who, for whatever reason, do not realize the amazing gift they've been given at birth, hope is not lost. The gift is still there, God does not take it back. Perhaps as a youth, or later as an adult, even at an advanced age, something, a life experience, an encounter with an influential person in their life, something they read, may prompt them to recognize and explore the gift. At first it may not appear to be anything special, which can sometimes be the case with some of the gifts anyone receives. That is, until one realizes who the gift is from.

Suddenly it's not so much the gift, as it is the one who gives it and the meaning and intent in which it is given.

Every gift from God is a blessing. It is the way in which God takes a proactive role in our lives. It is the way God teaches us, instructs us, and shows us the way, all the while keeping His eyes upon us and watching over us. Life is never without challenges, obstacles, bends in the road, and hills to climb. Through the Spirit within, God is there to be our guide, our friend, our confidant who will see us through the most challenging of times. Whether from a very early age, or later in life, appreciating this gift of God's love, one is certain to live a fulfilling and rewarding life.

PLANTED TO GROW

When a person in agriculture, a gardener, or even a little child plants a seed in soil, they "Plant it to Grow" into whatever it is meant to be, which may be a source of food, a flower, tree, or some other type of plant or vegetation. The sower waits with anticipation to see the seed sprout, while providing water and nutrients, as it pushes through the soil and gradually develops and grows to maturity. Of all who plant, the child is the most intent, returning frequently to see if the seed is growing, then being delighted with its progress. No one plants a seed in soil without having the desire for it to spring forth and grow to its full development and potential. As plants mature and produce the bountiful harvest intended, they reward and glorify the sower for the efforts and care given.

God plants the seed of the Holy Spirit in every human being at the moment of inception. That seed is planted with God having the desire to see it grow and develop into a beautiful person whose heart and soul are filled with love and peace. Like the sower of seeds, God also waits and watches with anticipation like the child, returning frequently to see if the seed is growing, and is delighted with its progress. God's seed is not just any seed, but like the sower's, His seed is planted in order to mature into a person who has specific talents and skills. God nourishes that seed with blessings of opportunities for developing into a fully mature and productive person.

Just as elements may slow the progress of growth and development in a plant or even result in its wilting or dying, elements of society and the world around may cause a decline, reversal in the growth and development, or even the death of a person. Yet God stands prepared to protect, restore, and provide divine intervention in a person's life to overcome all adversity.

While a plant may only subtly indicate its needs for survival, a person is able to reach out to God in prayer. When crying out in a loud voice, the grace of God will provide the way in trial and tribulation and be a beacon of hope guiding one through the greatest challenge.

God does not plant seeds only to wither and die unproductively and without being a shining example of His love. God plants the seed of the Holy Spirit in a person to grow, develop, mature, and shine forth. It is through living with an awakened power of the Holy Spirit within, and fulfilling the purpose we've been gifted to manifest, that we glorify God for His blessing of the Holy Spirit that He "Planted to Grow".

MORNING GLORIES

Most people simply believe that a morning glory is noted for merely opening up in the early hours of the day when the sun comes up, looks pretty all day long, and at the end of a long day just closes up to await another sunrise.

It certainly does that. However, watching the area around the morning Glories during the day one will quickly realize that there is a buzz of activity around morning glories all day long. Butterflies flutter in and out as bees' hover about partaking of the sweet nectar to make honey. Birds fly by as other animals seem to wander about enjoying the wonder and the beauty of it all.

As we open our eyes to a new day, we are blessed when we embrace it with a happy heart and a smiling face all aglow like the morning glory. We can be assured that God has set aside the things of the past, and we may do so also. Each day we are born anew. We are prepared to follow where the Spirit leads. As we move about our day, in the same way the morning glory encounters all that nature has to offer, we readily and enthusiastically interact with others throughout our day.

That is, if we choose to do so. Sometimes we may not feel enthusiastic about opening our eyes to the things we may face in this new day that is before us. We may not feel the joy of a happy heart and having to deal with others may be threatening and repulsive. The thought of the challenges and pitfalls we are certain we will encounter discourages us from even wanting to venture out. Better that we should close the door on the world and just crawl back into our safe space.

In the same way the morning glory is awakened by the sun, nourished by the fruits of the earth and gentle rains provided by God, we are blessed by "The Awakening of the Power of the Holy Spirit Within." With God there to guide us, through the Spirit Within, we are able to open our lives up to the world around us. We are eager to greet others with a happy and joyful attitude. We forge forward meeting challenges and bumps in the road aggressively and with a positive attitude.

When our day is done, as the morning glory quietly and peacefully closes for the night, we are also prepared to relax, reminisce about the blessings of the day, and praise God for giving us the privilege of experiencing the wonder of His creation.

". . . I focus on one thing: forgetting the past and looking forward to what lies ahead." Philippians 3:13 (NLT)

Thank you, Lord, for morning Glories!

LOST IN FLINT

"When about eight or nine years old, a trip to the city of Flint with an aunt and cousins to visit relatives became a clear indication what in future years would expose me for who I am an indignant, stubborn, and strong-minded individual determined to face the world on my terms no matter what".

It was a warm summer day and I walked with my cousins, generally older than I, several city blocks from the relative's house to an ice cream parlor. Upon returning to the relative's house we came upon a point where the sidewalks, parallel to the street, offered an alternate direction in the form of a Y that could be taken. The cousins insisted that one of the ways was the way back to the house we had come from. Thinking they were not being honest and trying to fool me, and being sure I remembered we had come the other way, they went their way and I went mine.

Four hours later I continued aimlessly wandering about the neighborhood hopelessly lost. Fortunately, having walked around the same block several times, a retired police officer, who had been sitting on his front porch, recognized this hopeless, crying, lost soul who had passed in front of his house a couple of times. He sent his wife to ask what my name was and what the problem was. Calling the local precinct and learning my aunt had reported me missing, a patrol car soon arrived, and the officer drove me to the relative's house.

What is your attitude about life? Are you indignant, stubborn, and strong minded, determined to face the world on your own terms no matter what, while turning your back on God and the clear direction He has for your life? If so, you may find yourself wondering aimlessly, not knowing where you are or how to get to where you need to be. God is there watching. He sees the fear, anxiety, and frustration you're experiencing. He will also send help when you're in a time of distress. By His Holy Hand through the Awakened Power of the Holy Spirit Within, you will be picked up and taken to where you belong.

ISOLATED

A person can be Isolated from others from time to time and survive, but never from God.

There may be times in one's life when they become separated from loved ones, other family members, and even from friends and acquaintances. At times like this the person may feel alone, left out, and lonely. These periods are generally for short periods and may be caused by uncontrollable circumstances. Divorce, illness, hospitalization, and occupational changes are a few of the more likely causes where a person may find themselves Isolated from others. Making amends where necessary, meeting new acquaintances, having new associates, and creating new friends soon removes one from the isolation and life moves on.

Having a meaningful relationship with God overshadows the difficult times when a person feels and, in fact, is Isolated from others. In the silence of the Holy Spirit of God, a person experiences the peaceful calm that provides wellbeing, peace, and a connection to the brotherhood of man. Being isolated from God is entirely different. Despair, fear, rejection, self-doubt, and so much more may cause one to take desperate steps to mask, overcome, and attempt to alleviate these negative feelings and emotions. A person may resort to excessiveness, mind-alternating substances, physical harm, and even suicide.

God is an ever-present source of companionship. A strong ally always ready to be loving, compassionate, and a true source of friendship. Loved ones, family, friends, and others may come and go, but God is always there for you. Call upon Him, for He will hear you and beckon to your call.

THE LANDING

MWD—Landing: a level part of a staircase (as at the end of a flight of stairs)

A landing on a stairway, staircase, or stairwell, depending on what a person may prefer to refer to it as, is a level area generally somewhere in the middle of the stairs between two different levels of a building, house, or some other structure. The stairs generally extending up or down from the landing go in a different direction, anywhere from a few degrees to ninety degrees. To leave the landing one must therefore proceed upward or downward from their position on the stairs.

One might first consider how they got there. Was it by coming up or were they going down? Then decide, is it their desire and intention to continue in that direction, or are they headed in a direction where they will be unable to find what it was they intended to find? Do they wish to return to where they came from, or do they wish to avoid returning to that position or level and whatever it was that they had left behind?

As one surveys their options, looking up they may be looking at a hallway with closed doors, which, if the person has not been in the place before, they will likely have no idea what lies behind any of the doors. They may speculate that there is a bedroom or a bathroom, but until they ascend to the top of the stairs and open the doors, it remains an uncertainty and only speculation. Likewise, as the person contemplates looking at going down, if they have come from a specific direction, i.e. from an entrance door to the structure, they have no idea exactly what else they will find down the halls that lead from the bottom of the stairs.

Again, speculation may be that there is a kitchen, living or family room, and perhaps even another bedroom, but until they descend to the bottom of the stairs and begin to explore that level of the building, it is only speculation. Of course, we're assuming it is a residential house to begin with.

Consequently, one might ask, "What is it I wish to find or do?" Each direction offers rooms that provide different opportunities.

In life a person may sometimes find themselves in a situation such as being on a landing questioning themselves whether they should go up or down. From one's position, what lies beyond the path ahead may be obscured and unknown. They may question, "Is this path taking me on an upward journey, or am I on a downward spiral headed in a direction I wish to avoid returning to? However, when you willingly release yourself to the purposeful plan God has for your life, He will guide you. The important thing to do is just move off the landing. Through the Power of the Awakened Spirit of God within, you will be guided in following the direction that is going to lead you to the destiny God has in His plan for your life.

If you have chosen the wrong direction to go, God will point out the error of your choice and redirect you. If you have doubts, fears, or hesitations about the direction you are taking, set them aside and continue to proceed in faith and confidence that only good can be on and along the path you have chosen. God's plan for each of our lives is one where we will find fulfillment, joy, and serenity. It is the relationship one shares with God that assures them that they have made the right choices. Serious doubts are a sure indication that your relationship with God needs some serious attention.

Build upon that relationship through prayer and medication and Get Off That Landing.

GO AHEAD—REBEL

God has all the time in the world.

God will still be there when you hit the wall.

He'll still be a helping hand to see you through.

God still loves you no matter what you have done

or what you are doing.

He still wants to be your friend, a true companion.

God will not judge you, He will heal you.

God will not belittle you, He will give you

self-assurance.

He will not beat you down, He will build you up.

God wants you to be whole, strong, fulfilled,

and joyful.

Turn to God, He will answer your call and be

there for you.

Go ahead, be a rebel, God will still be

there for you.

CLEARING THE WAY

In snow country, on mornings after several inches of snow have fallen, driving on a road that has been cleared of snow and ice, one is aware that earlier it was a snowplow that had cleared the path. Perhaps, just ahead and out of sight, there is a big truck with a plow pushing snow to the side of the road and spreading salt or a liquid to keep the road from freezing. A person has confidence, even though they can't see them, that the road crews are out making the path, which they are following, safe and trouble free.

The snowplow may encounter deep snow and, at times, drifting snow piled high ahead of it, yet it isn't deterred and plows through it clearing the way. It may, however, leave a thin layer of snow covering the road that may cause you to be cautious and drive more carefully. At the same time, the deep snow that could cause you to stop, get stuck, or even have an accident has been moved out of the way.

Likewise, faith in God works in the same way. Even though you can't see what God is doing, you trust that God is out there ahead of you clearing the path ahead. God knows the difficulties and problems you may encounter on your path of life. Through faith, we acknowledge and believe that God will reduce all obstacles, big and small, to little or nothing, making the way safe and secure.

At times God may allow circumstances to cause us to slow down and be cautious in order to avoid a catastrophic situation. Remaining in faith that God is leading the way ahead of us will keep us safe from harm and from being involved in problematic events in our life. It is important to understand that "While we can't see God, we'll feel His presence" and know that He's somewhere out there making our way clear.

FILL THE GAP

A person may wonder and ask, "Why does God favor one person and yet appear to turn His back on another?" Why this gap? What is so different between one person and another? The difference between one being apparently shunned and another being favored by God is simply in the relationship a person seeks and maintains with God. Whether the relationship is a result of a person committing themselves to God or through the intercessory prayer of another on the behalf of someone, God favors that person.

God has given every individual the free choice to ignore him, take Him for granted and fail to recognize His role in their life, or consciously and purposefully include God in their life. Including God in one's life opens the pathway that fills the gap. God's desire is to have an open and committed relationship with every person. Unfortunately not every person has the desire or seeks to have a relationship with God. Yet they are inclined to ask, "Why do others always appear to be so blessed and favored by God?"

It's the gap. Fill the gap by developing an active relationship with God, and you will begin to see ways in which God works in your life. It generally starts with little things. Stop and think, was that evening out for dinner with a friend or loved one pleasant or a disaster? It doesn't matter if it was a fast-food restaurant or one that is elegant. Was the service good, the food satisfying, and the bill what you expected? Maybe God had something to do with it. Otherwise, everything, or at least something significant, may have gone wrong or have been very displeasing.

Even when we do our best to try to maintain our relationship with God and fill that gap, things can go wrong. That is when God really steps up to favor us. It is in these situations that God gives us patience, understanding, and the ability to let it go and move on. When we are able to see how God works in our lives in areas of little consequence or importance, we realize how important having filled that gap and built that relationship is when we are faced with major and consequential circumstances that could be life changing. We should never overlook a situation, no matter how small or large, where God has taken an active role in our lives.

It is equally important to be an intercessor in prayer for others. Whether it's a loved one, friend, or even a total stranger who in some way comes to our attention and needs the favor of God in their life. Sometimes we can be the bridge that spans that gap that will result in developing a significant and lasting relationship between that person and God. Surely it will strengthen our relationship with God as well.

"Fill the Gap"

MANIPULATION

(a blessing or a curse?)

DEF: MWD—Manipulate: to control or play upon by
artful, unfair, or insidious means
especially to one's own advantage.
To change by artful or unfair means so
as to serve one's purpose

MWD—Influence: a: the act or power of
producing an effect without apparent
exertion of force or exercise of command.
b: corrupt interference with
authority for personal gain

One that exerts influence. The power or
capacity of causing an effect in direction or
in intangible ways (sway)

God has given every person the gift of, and ability, to be influential
with others.

However, do we influence people as God would have us, by being an influence in their lives by advocating peace, love, joy, and fulfillment? Or, do
we influence others for our personal gain through greed, jealousy, and
arrogance?

The life of Jesus Christ set the perfect example of God's intention as to the
manner in which we should strive to be an influence on others.

Manipulation is a strong term, one that oftentimes carries a negative connotation. Yet God gave each person, to one degree or another, the ability
to manipulate, or if you prefer influence others. Manipulation is a strong
and effective ability. It can be used to strengthen people and guide them

to being a better person, or it can demean a person and put them down. Manipulation to make one appear better or more important than another is not the way in which God intended for us to have influence over others. Manipulation to raise a person above self-doubt and inferiority is the type of influence and the reason God gave us this ability. It is the example that Christ epitomized through His life and interaction with others while on this earth.

We have to ask ourselves as well, "Am I being manipulated by others?" The fact is you are. The question to ask yourself is, "Is it to your advantage or decimation?" Every day, communication and interaction with others have an influence on our lives. TV, other news outlets, and social media are a big part of our lives. Are we allowing what we hear, read, and see manipulate our thinking and behavior in a positive or negative way? Do we take what we are exposed to at face value, or do we evaluate it according to our core beliefs and moral values? We cannot escape the fact that there are situations out there that have the desire to manipulate us in accepting their ideals, theories, and standards. However, are they consistent with our goals and objectives in life. Do they coincide and support the life God has in His plan for us to live as we encounter our day-to-day routines?

If a person is going to be manipulated, let God be the manipulator, let the life of Jesus Christ be the influencer, let those with whom you share principles and ideals pleasing to God be the ones you are manipulated by. In that way, the influence and the way in which you manipulate others will strengthen their relationship with God and yours as well.

A blessing or a curse? An influence on others for personal gain through greed, jealousy, and arrogance, or an advocate of peace, love, joy, and fulfillment?

EVER PRESENT
EVER AVAILABLE

It is not a matter of whether or not God is willing to be a part of our lives. The question is, "Are we willing to open our hearts, minds, and souls to God and release ourselves to God"? It's not God who is judging us; it's our tyrannical mind that espouses guilt, wrongdoing, and fear.

God has already set aside the past and is there to guide us in a new direction. Are we willing to release ourselves to the new and set aside the things of the past?

Friends may choose to come and go; it is their decision. However, a relationship with God is not one that God chooses whether or not to have with us. God's decision is to be an everlasting part of our lives. To be "EVER PRESENT—EVER AVAILABLE." It is our decision to accept God, His friendship, love, compassion, and the clear direction He has for our lives

THE "MODEL TRAIN" WRECK OF LIFE

If you're at all familiar with having run a model train as a child, you'll no doubt remember when you, or someone else (-: perhaps that nasty brother :-) ran the engine and a set of cars around an oval or round track. It always seemed that the engine and the cars following had to be run faster and faster until the engine went sailing off the track, taking several cars with it in a massive wreck and pileup. With that, the engine was picked up, anything broken or bent was repaired, and the engine was gently placed back on the track with the wheels carefully set and aligned on the track, followed by each car that had fallen by the wayside. With that, the train was started back around the track, sometimes, being operated gently and in a more moderate way.

So it is in life sometimes. Just as if you were there to pick up the engine and get it straightened out to run again, God is there to pick us up. Through His grace He straightens us out and fixes any bent or broken parts of our lives. He's there to set us back on the clear track He has for our lives. Circumstances can sometimes leave us broken, bent, and off track. However, a loving, compassionate God of miracles and restoration wants to help us set aside the things of the past. It is God's desire through His grace to see each and every one of us back on track.

Praise God and allow Him to guide you.

VARIABLE SPEED

There are many things that are operable at available speeds. Kitchen appliances, such as mixers, shop tools such as drills, windshield wipers on vehicles and more. There are specific advantages for having the ability to manually, or through automation, vary the speed of numerous things to maximize the efficiency of their operation in various situations.

As an example, in light rain, there is no need for vehicle windshield wipers to operate in a rapid fashion back and forth to remove the rain from the windshield to provide good vision. While in heavy rain the faster movement is required to keep the windshield clear. The adjustability provides for the most favorable result. It is our personal experience and, in many cases, that of others through things such as instruction manuals, which guide us in adjusting the variable options while using a particular item in order to operate it most efficiently in a specific situation.

Our relationship with God is generally also "Variable Speed". When things are running smoothly, we may tend to slow down our communication and awareness of God and the role God is taking in our lives. Like the windshield wipers in light rain, with circumstances in life being somewhat routine and considered light in nature, we may be inclined to take God for granted. When things become heaver like the rain and more burdensome, we're quick to speed up the pace of our relationship with God, just as we would increase the intensity of the windshield wipers.

God's desire is not to be "Variable Speed". God is willing and desirous to run full speed in all circumstances and in every variable we face in life. We don't have to worry about whether we need to turn God on manually or have God involved automatically depending on the experiences we are facing.

By keeping God in the forefront of our lives, in full speed, whatever we are confronted with will be handled appropriately. By continually acknowledging and praising God in all things, we keep God operating at full speed in our lives. We need not be concerned with dialing up the proper "Variable Speed" to seek God's intervention in the circumstances in our life. God is there, operating at full speed and at maximum capacity.

DETOUR

Road commissions are generally good at putting up signs that direct people in taking an alternate route when the main road becomes unpassable. Sometimes the detour will route people along back roads and through unfamiliar territory. This can sometimes become confusing, and if the signage directing the route is insufficient or unclear, a person can become lost if they take a wrong turn. Otherwise, the new route may provide a pleasant experience exploring an area one would otherwise never have ventured through.

At times in our lives, we may find the path we are on blocked and unpassable. There may not be obvious signs directing us on an alternate course in order to continue on our journey of life pursuing a particular objective or goal. One may experience frustration if they begin to realize the path which they were certain was the perfect one to take and pursue, the one which their lives was to be part of, has become unattainable and one of destruction. Confusion, hesitation, despair, and even trauma may result in and/or provoke illness or life-threatening circumstances.

Living with the awareness of God within offers the assuredness that one will be guided in following the path by which they will fulfill God's purpose and plan for their life. They may resist an alternate objective and particularly the apparent paths necessary to follow. Even so, to resist the negative impact of the situation and to move on with faith in God's guiding hand, one will have the assurance that by this detour in life they will be diligently guided to this new destiny through the Spirit within.

Yes, there will be times that doubt, hesitation, and confusion will result in not recognizing or understanding the signs given. However, his new path and destination being followed may just be an exciting serendipitous experience that is far more rewarding and pleasant than what would have been experienced on the original path and objective being pursued.

INFLUENTIAL

A person is far more influential with where they are at, and what they are doing, than where they have been and what they have done. Besides themselves, the only people who are impressed with what they've done and where they've been are generally the people who wish they had been there or had done that themselves.

Living in the past restricts us from progressing on the path God intends for us to follow. It limits us to the level of achievement we already know we can accomplish and are comfortable with. Rather than considering oneself to be at the beginning, or at least in the middle of the journey, where the opportunity for greater and more fulfilling experiences are achievable.

When one climbs a mountain, or hikes the trail to the top of a hill, when the top is reached, there is that short time and period of exhilaration of having accomplished the journey. As one looks about, absorbs the wonder of where they are and where they've been and what they've achieved, that feeling soon becomes diminished. As boredom with where they are settles in, the sight of higher mountains in the distance calls. The thoughts and realization of what comes next settle in. Generally, it means descending to another level well below the pinnacle they have reached.

While a person may be saying to others, "Look at me," they are far more influential when they say, "Follow me," and even more pleasing to God and fulfilling of His plan for their life when they say, "Join me as we climb this mountain together."

While past experiences and achievements are certainly a thing to be proud of in some cases, and perhaps in others regret, they are what has shaped the person we are. Treating them as an influence to where we are going, rather than as something one has achieved, they can and should be considered as the chapters in a book yet to be finished.

ACHIEVEMENTS
"Pie in the Sky"

How one feels about their achievements at a given point in their life may be disappointing. Perhaps there have been missed goals, projects abandoned, undone, or left incomplete. Everyone has dreams, intentions, goals, and objectives. Some are common things we more or less expect to realize and accomplish. Such as simply making it through the routine of the day, achieving a certain educational level, becoming employed and making a sustainable living. Other objectives can be more challenging and difficult to accomplish, such as the "Pie in the Sky" ideas and pursuits.

One's feelings about their achievements may also be influenced by others. This may cause a person to become so intent on pleasing others and their expectations that they may lose focus on the achievements they themselves have made. These are the accomplishments that do correspond to and are a result of the application of the talents, skills, knowledge, and educational level of an individual. In other words, one may find themselves over their head trying to do things they aren't really qualified for, consequently being self-judging that they are incompetent and a failure.

Regardless, while at times we may feel disillusioned with our level of accomplishments, it is important to stop and take note of the fact that there may be certain outstanding things God has used our lives for. We may not have any idea how God may have changed another's life through some little thing we have done; an act of kindness, a complement, a seemingly insignificant helping hand, a friendly smile. There are certainly times when gestures of these types by others have influenced our lives.

The important thing is not to stop dreaming and having the desire to reach those "Pie in the Sky" goals. God isn't done with you as long as you're present on His good earth. God plants the seeds of greatness in every person. How and when that seed will spring forth, and what it will manifest itself as, is something only God knows.

God doesn't give up on the way in which He intends to use the talents and skills He has given us. We cannot give up on ourselves, and we certainly must never give up on God.

QUIET THE TYRANNICAL MIND

Anything and everything good done by
anyone has, is, and always will be by the
Awakened Spirit of God within.

Anything and everything evil done by
anyone has, is, and
always will be by the expression of the
Tyrannical Mind.

The Awakened Spirit within Quiets the
Tyrannical Mind!

CHANGE

If we are praying and waiting for God to do something in our lives, perhaps it is God who is being patient and waiting for us to make a change before He can do what it is that we are praying for Him to do.

If one is praying for God to resolve a health issue, to cure a devastating disease, to provide rapid healing of an injury, or whatever it may be, perhaps God is waiting for you to make a life-changing commitment to alter or change your lifestyle or a certain habit.

If one is praying for God to provide for financial help or recovery, perhaps God is waiting for you to be less careless with spending, the use of credit, or seeking after material things that may not be necessary.

If one is praying for God to resolve a relationship issue or to introduce you to that person you have drempt would be the love of your life, perhaps God is waiting for you to make a life-changing commitment by changing your circle of friends, personal habits, or some other factor that is preventing God from granting your prayerful petition.

Granted, if we keep praying without doing our part, sooner or later it will force God's hand. His only resource for convincing us to be prepared for the answer to our prayer may be a drastic, and/or at the very least, an uncomfortable move or change.

UNEXPECTED CONSEQUENCES

There are some stores today, that use shopping carts for customers to gather the items they desire to purchase, which have little lock boxes attached to the cart with a chain that attaches one cart to another, requiring a coin to be inserted in the box to release the cart so the customer is able to use it as they shop. The intent on the part of the store, in addition to other practical reasons, is to reduce and potentially eliminate the expense of hiring employees to corral the carts left in a parking lot, after customers remove their purchases and abandon the cart, and return them to the store.

Consequently, if the customer wants their coin back, they have to return the cart to a central location, generally near the entrance of the store. They must push their cart into another, then in order to retrieve their coin, they have to plug the linking chain from the cart theirs is shoved into in the little box on the cart they are returning. This is a practical idea on the part of the store, and customers are willing to be cooperative because the store involved is generally thought to save the customer money by being able to offer lower prices because of this and other cost-saving measures.

A very interesting thing occurs very often at these locations. As one customer empties their shopping cart into their vehicle, another customer preparing to enter the store will offer to return the cart to the store in order to use it for their shopping convenience. This also saves the first customer the trip back to the front of the store from the location of their vehicle in the parking lot. The second customer, of course, offers the first customer the coin they would otherwise have to use anyway to get a cart to do their shopping.

Unexpected consequences? While the store management may think their prime intention is to save money, the consequences are the good will and friendliness that result in the exchange between customers. In many situations, when the second customer offers to give the first customer a coin in reimbursement, the first customer may not accept the coin, indicating that the previous customer had given them the cart without accepting the coin. With that, the second customer responds with a thankful and friendly attitude, saying, "Then I'll pass the gesture on to the next", and so it goes. The brief uplifting, good feeling exchange between strangers is suddenly an "Unexpected Consequence."

God provides us with many opportunities in our daily life to interact with others in order to be brotherly and to demonstrate fellowship, concern, be helpful, and in some cases even be an inspiration. The shopping cart situation is one of the more obvious ways, but God gives us subtle opportunities as well when we are awakened to the power of the Holy Spirit within. Responding may not only be a blessing to another, it just may bless us in a totally "Unexpected" way. You know, or at least you will learn, that's the way God works!

REARVIEW MIRROR

How often, when driving, does something catch your eye, and not being sure of exactly what it was, or if it actually was even there, you check the "Rearview Mirror"? It's just a glance as you concentrate on what's ahead and what you're currently passing. At times you may ask yourself, "Should I turn around and go back"? I think perhaps I missed something very interesting and important."

It's much like that with the many blessings with which God fills our lives. We find ourselves looking back and asking, "What just happened"? Did an extraordinary event just take place that I didn't even notice until after it had happened"? Like driving, we seldom turn and go back. Instead, we refocus and concentrate on where we are and where we are going. So often, concerned with our destination, we fail to recognize and appreciate the present as it passes by so quickly. Is that always so necessary?

Perhaps from time to time we need to slow down and imagine we're on the scenic drive of life. Taking a scenic drive in the country or an area surrounded by nature we're inclined to take our time. We may even stop from time to time to observe the beauty of God's gift to us. The many blessings in our lives are the scenic aspect of the path in life we're taking. We need to take time to recognize them and praise God for His goodness and for these blessings. In which case, instead of looking in the "Rearview Mirror", we may find ourselves experiencing the many blessings in our life in real time.

RELATIONSHIP

Nothing in this world is more important than a personal relationship with God. It is through the "Awakened Power of The Holy Spirit Within" that the purpose and meaning of life unfolds. It is the point when life ceases to be a challenge and becomes an opportunity for the unexpected, raising us to our highest level.

Through a personal relationship with God, the oneness we experience elevates to a friendship, companionship, and ever presence. One's faith in God not only becomes enduring, but the faith in oneself is bolstered and fortified.

We notice things, which once were taken for granted, and see the beauty and awesomeness of all that God has created around us. We pursue tasks, even those considered menial, with enthusiasm and strive for excellence in all we do. Our every action and response is shrouded with appreciation and thanksgiving.

A personal relationship with God goes beyond prayer and becomes an ongoing and open source of communication. By the acceptance of God's ever presence one hears and understands when God speaks. The awareness of God's communication affirms what it is, that it is, that it is yours to do. The grace of God provides the ability and courage to see it through.

"If I take the wings of the morning and settle at the farthest limits of the sea, even there your hand shall lead me, and your right hand shall hold me fast." *Psalm 139:9–10 (ESV)*

STAND FIRM

On a recent visit to the Great Smokey Mountain National Park, I was blessed to have an encounter with wildlife that was a totally and unexpected serendipitous event.

I had spent a couple of days in the area with a friend spending time driving along nature preserves in the park enjoying the wonder of God's amazing creation. The mountains that rise majestically in multiple forms, the trees and shrubbery that grace the landscape in colorful and abundant display, the rocky streams and graceful waterfalls that thrive with the ever abundant supply of water. And, the occasional, on this trip the very occasional, wild animal that wonders near enough to see, appreciate, and possibly capture a picture of.

Upon leaving the park to drive home, it was suggested that we take a side trip to an area in the National Park where elk had been reintroduced a few years earlier, with the hope that we could see them in their natural setting. The road to get there was a harrowing experience in itself. Once off the main route the approximate ten-mile narrow one-lane gravel road was a bumpy ride and challenging as it wound up and over a mountain. Offering spectacular views overlooking steep drop-offs, it added moments of adventure, not to mention apprehension when approached by an oncoming vehicle.

Having reached the valley in which the elks were supposed to have been seen in the past, we parked at the edge of a large field. A wooded area stood several hundred yards from our location with the mountainside rising up beyond. With binoculars we were able to locate a small number of elk in a herd at the edge of that wooded area. We watched in awe, as there was some movement that we were able to capture from that distance on camera.

After spending some time at that spot, without seeing any additional activity, we decided to leave the area and continue our journey home.

Leaving, because of the narrow road, I decided to drive the hundred yards or so an area where it would be more convenient to turn around to drive out of the park. However, as I reached the turnaround area, we realized that we could get a better view of the elk we had been watching and parked to get out to perhaps get some better pictures. Mind you, there were several signs warning to "Stay Back 50 Feet from the Elk."

We were only there a few minutes when not only the elk we had been watching began to move about, but others, presumably of the same herd, started to come out of a wooded area just to the left of where we were located and not much more than the fifty feet from us. There were older as well as younger elk in this group, with the much larger bull elk remaining in the initial area where we had first observed the animals. A few of these closer to us headed across the road to the stream behind us and crossed fairly close while still maintaining their distance from the handful of people and the few cars that were parked in the area.

My friend had walked up a short trail that led into the woods and upon returning, told me an elk was coming down the trail. As I stood near the trail next to a wooded area, a female elk came sauntering along the trail and up to where I was standing holding my camera and taking her picture. She stopped just a few feet from me, and as I stood motionless with my camera rolling, she looked me up and down, glanced to the rear and all around, looked back at me, took a good smell of me, and sauntered off to join the other elk.

The experience was emotional and truly a serendipitous event. A special blessing to stand so close to one of God's beautiful creatures. Her mane was beautiful and appeared soft, much like that of a retriever I had lost a couple of years earlier. Her coat was a beautiful soft cropped light brown, her head was that of a proud animal with big beautiful eyes and large nostrils that expanded wide to get the full scent of this two-legged beast that was watching and taking a picture of her.

After watching the others in the herd for a little while longer, we left the area and headed out of the park, where we encountered several turkeys pecking their delight in the field close to the road.

It took a few days for me to fully appreciate the encounter. To really feel and understand it in a way that I might appreciate what a blessing it was, and perhaps a lesson that God was using to get my attention. Daily it is my intention to release myself to the power of the Holy Spirit within to fulfill God's plan for my life. Standing still, much more, "Standing Firm" is challenging. The tyrannical mind has thoughts of its own and challenges God's will for one's life every step of the way. Standing Firm, letting go, trusting God, and believing that God will provide our every need at the right time and in the right way assures us that He will bless us in ways we could never have imagined we would be blessed. I never imagined I would encounter this beautiful and awesome animal so closely, and in such an emotional and personal way.

MAGIC

A favorite magic trick the majority of magicians seem to use in their act is pulling something from the sleeve on their arm. Everything from endless scarves to doves and nearly everything one can imagine. Such a popular and identifiable trick, it has come to be known as a reference people use to question something someone is hiding from others. It often prompts the comment, "What do you have up your sleeve"? It may be that the person has been doing something, or at least preparing to do something, while being unwilling to let others know about it. While at the same time, others suspect that something is up, "THEIR SLEEVE"!!

Sounds like something one may wonder or even ask God about. What's up, God? God doesn't do magic, but God is a miracle worker. Like the magician though, God may have something pertaining to one's life, Up His Sleeve. What it is, how big it is, how many of whatever it is there are, like the magician, no one knows until He determines it is the right time for it to be exposed. There are times in a person's life that they may become restless, uncomfortable as to where they are, or the amount of time it is taking to progress in a life situation that they may wish to improve upon or move beyond. One may ask, "God, why aren't You answering my prayers? Why must I endure this situation? Why, God, Why?

Well, perhaps God has something up His sleeve that He is prepared to do in their life that is far more surprising, rewarding, and fulfilling than anything they may imagine. No, it's not about magic, it's all about a loving, compassionate, miracle-working God of restoration. It's all about a God with perfect timing. A good magician knows exactly when to expose what it is that will be a surprise when it is pulled from the sleeve, in order to make the audience "Ooooo" and "Aaaaa" at the magician's cunning ability to surprise and do the seeming impossible. Almighty God knows exactly what, when, and why to bring to fruition the things in a person's life that will leave them in awe with God's ability to shower seeming impossible blessings upon their life. Particularly in times when whatever it is, is needed and appreciated the most.

BLESSED BY GOD

I AM BLESSED BY GOD

IN MORE WAYS

THAN MY HEART WILL EVER BEAT

IN MY ENTIRE LIFETIME

IN FACT

EACH HEARTBEAT IS A BLESSING

IN AND OF ITSELF

FOCUS

Every moment of our lives we are FOCUSED on something. Whether trivial or significant and consequential, something we are intensely concentrating on, or we are simply somewhat unmindful about. In every situation we seek a result, a consequence, effect, or an outcome.

It may be personal satisfaction, a health issue, materialistic gain, or perhaps elevated life status. It may have to do with our life situation or that of another. Realizing or attaining the desired result can be satisfying and rewarding. In certain situations, the desired results can be anticlimactic, discouraging, and even devastating.

Suppose however, that whatever the quest we were pursuing, or whatever it had to do with, was FOCUSED on fulfilling God's plan for our life. Not on what we wanted, but on what God intended for us to achieve to fulfill His plan. It's not what we are doing or striving for that is important. It's not how much or what we could buy materialistically as a result of a monetary achievement, through work, an investment, or even winning a lottery. These things may motivate and encourage us, but once achieved, they likely leave us empty and unfulfilled only to pursue and chase a new idea or dream. It's what we're FOCUSED on.

When we are faced with negativism, lack of satisfaction, or evil in life, we must FOCUS on pleasing God, and then the grace of God will pour out upon us and quiet the tyrannical mind that manifests these fears and concerns. Rather than FOCUSING on what we want or the pleasure we seek, FOCUSING on how what we are doing will glorify God puts everything in a whole different perspective. Menial tasks become meaningful, difficult situations become less challenging, hopeless situations become attainable. FOCUSED on how that same effort we've been putting into personal and material gain will fulfill God's plan and glorify God for the blessings in our lives will provide peace, joy, and fulfillment.

It may even result in even greater rewards in every way, than we could ever have imagined we could expect to accomplish or achieve. God favors those who are FOCUSED on pleasing Him, whatever they do, no matter how trivial or significant. Rather than being FOCUSED on whatever it is that our efforts may achieve or even on the blessings God has bestowed upon us in our lives, FOCUS on the God who blessed you and how we are glorifying God through the efforts we put forth.

BINOCULARS

When using binoculars, we focus them to see better what we see though them. What we are actually looking at though is simply an instrument made of a hard material such as plastic with glass lenses. An object we see through the lenses of the binoculars may be made to be seen closer and more distinguishable, but in reality, we are just looking at the lenses. In other words, we're looking at an instrument, or the parts of that instrument. Removing the instrument, the binoculars, we may not be able to see an object at all, or at least not in a way for it to be distinguishable.

So, when someone looks at us, is what they are looking at what they are really seeing? Are they just seeing an individual as though looking at the plastic body of the binoculars with eyes as lenses? Or, are they seeing through all that and seeing a child of God? Looking through binoculars a person may see a beautiful bird souring among the clouds. Perhaps in a distance one will see nothing but trees and shrubs, but through the binoculars will get a glimpse of some sort of wildlife such as a wild deer or bear.

Awakened to the Holy Spirit within and Releasing Ourselves Willingly and Purposefully to God's will for our lives, we won't be seen simply as a person, but as an instrument through which the love of God will come into focus. We will be guided by God into situations where we are able to be helpful, compassionate, caring, loving, encouraging, and uplifting to others. In doing so, others will see through us, getting a glimpse of a child of God.

A person can be hard and impersonal with cold and rigid eyes. They may remain incased in their own world, just as one may leave binoculars in their case, never removing them to look through them to view the beauty they are able to reveal. God intended for us to be out in the open, to be used to focus on His love for mankind. At first what one sees when looking at us may be fuzzy and unrecognizable, but God has the ability to adjust the focus, revealing all the attributes He has bestowed upon you as His beautiful and Radiant child.

Free yourself of the encasement of the cold hard world in which you protect yourself. Let those with whom you associate see through that hard shell and blurry lens. Be the instrument exemplifying and being an amplification of the love of God!

EXPECTING TOO MUCH

Traveling anywhere, to work, to the store, or on a local or cross-country trip, we rely on signage to help us get to where we're going. Without signs, maps, and directional devices, we would lose our way, encounter mishaps, and perhaps never reach our destination.

Then why doesn't God provide us with more obvious signage, directions, and other divine devices to assist us in reaching our spiritual destination? Is God "Expecting Too Much"?

Certain religions advocate that writings contained in books (i.e., the Bible, the Book of Mormon, the Qur'an, and others) contain all the guidance we need if we read them and follow their teachings. Yet to some, they seem to be vague and certainly not as direct as looking at a road sign with specific directions as to the way we need to go to get to our destination.

Is God "Expecting Too Much"? The revelation and answer to this question is in one simple yet awesome word, "Faith". When we have faith in God, and in fact in ourselves in trusting that God has blessed us with all we need to fulfill His plan for our lives, faith assures us that God will keep us on the right path to reach our spiritual destiny. God only asks and expects us to believe in Him and have faith in Him and His love for us.

Is that "Expecting Too Much"?

"TO BE" – "BECAUSE"

Do not try to live a life pleasing to God *"To Be"* blessed. Rather, Live a life of praise and thanksgiving while endeavoring to be an instrument of God's *love* and *peace, "Because"* you've been blessed.

Many times, in prayer or conversation with God, we ask to be blessed. We reason that God is a loving, giving, compassionate, and forgiving God. We may even make an attempt to negotiate with God in order *"To Be"* blessed.

The thing is, we are already blessed in so many ways! The very fact that we're alive, have a spiritual foundation for our lives, have good health or faith in God's miracle of healing are signs of His favor on us. Consider being able to sustain ourselves in order to nourish our bodies and have shelter with which to protect ourselves, these are gifts we have been blessed with. Is everything exactly the way we would like it to be? Do we face challenges in our spirituality, health, welfare, or even our desire to live a long life? More than likely! It is seldom in one's life that a person is able to say, "I'm exactly where I want to be, right here, right now, and have everything I could imagine I want or need, including health and resources."

Yet, there are ways in which God watches over us and does provide. There are ways we are blessed by God's proactive role in our lives. Sometimes we have to think back over time to recall the ways in which God took an active role in our lives and blessed us. The recollection of those times, the circumstances, the outcomes, will remind us that God has been faithful in the past and we have been blessed. *"Because"* we have been blessed, through a fundamental faith in God and His love for us, we have the reason to live a life of praise and thanksgiving while endeavoring to be an instrument of God's love and peace.

FUNNEL—JAR—BEADS

Take a jar, put the funnel in it, then pour the beads into the funnel and watch as the beads flow through the funnel into the jar. Simple, and yet the results are what one would expect. It all hinges on whether the funnel has a large-enough capacity for the size and shape of the beads and the jar has a wide-enough opening and capacity to accept the funnel and contain the number of beads that are to be funneled into the jar.

Stop and consider, the jar represents our lives, the beads represent everything we try to do in our lives, and the funnel, well . . . it could represent our mind, thoughts, desires, abilities, all of these, and more. Although, perhaps we should consider the funnel as being God, and instead of acting according to every whim and fancy, we should release ourselves to God and His will for our lives.

With God being the source which funnels everything into our lives, He will surly see that everything, every bead, is a perfect fit. Without the funnel, we may be inclined to attempt to shove all kinds of beads into our jar, even to the point of its overflowing and our being overwhelmed. With God being the funnel, large or improperly shaped beads for a person to have the ability to deal with in their lives; relationships, health issues, finances, and more will be held back by God. God will allow the funnel to plug up and prevent these from flowing through. When this happens, we may not be able to unplug the funnel, but God is able to extract these obstructions, allowing the free flow of what fits according to His plan for our lives. We need only call upon God and His compassionate love for every one of us to have our beads of life's difficult circumstances removed, thereby allowing our lives to continue to flow smoothly.

The jar? O' yes, that has a lot to do with it also. How big of a capacity do we have? Will God be confined to having to use a tiny funnel with tiny beads that, even then, will fill our jar of life and clog up the ability to pour in any additional beads (the blessings in our life).

God wants to fill our lives with abundant blessings of life, spirituality, health, and welfare. Do we approach life full of joy and with a positive attitude? Is our life open and our mind accepting of the Holy Spirit? Are we giving and loving towards others? Do we maintain a healthy lifestyle with proper foods and exercise? Are we conscientious about our finances and how we use the resources gifted to us by God? These are the things that determine the capacity of our jar.

Yes, the funnel—jar—and beads are one way to look at it. Perhaps a way we are able to ask God to guide us in examining our lives. A manner in which we may be better able to determine if we are fulfilling God's plan for our lives in order to find happiness and fulfillment. A thought process through which we may recognize the ways in which we are able to please and glorify God in thanksgiving for truly blessing us.

THANK YOU

Does God thank us? How does God thank us? What does God thank us for? Should we even expect God to thank us for anything? Are we ever, under any circumstances, deserving of a "Thank You" from God?

When we strive to pursue and maintain a growing and strong relationship with God, how does God respond? God says, "Thank You"! Yes, one may not look at it that way, but every blessing, every supernatural gift in seeing us through a difficult situation, every joy-filled moment, and every serendipitous event is a way in which God is saying, "Thank You". Yes, God does thank us!

How do we know if we, in fact, have collaborated with God in a way that we experience a mutual understanding and friendship with one another? How does God favor us? By being in relationship with God, He thanks us for that relationship. God gave us a free will. God did not insist or demand. God only gave us the opportunity. Our taking that opportunity is the very reason that God thanks us.

God has a certain plan for each of us to follow in our lives. It is a plan that fulfills His purpose for our lives, and a way in which we are able to glorify God through the way in which we live our lives. Releasing our lives to God, striving to do our best, setting aside our past mistakes and indiscretions are valid reasons to not only expect, but to acknowledge that God will thank us for our efforts.

Deserving? Well, that's another thing entirely! Nothing we could ever do, no good deed, no commitment, nothing, is able to declare or render us as being deserving. It is because God is a loving, compassionate, healing, restoring God, and a God of miracles that we can be assured that God will look upon us with understanding and favor. Therefore it is not us, it is God who is deserving! It is God to whom we need to say, "Thank You". Yes, God does respond to our relationship with Him and to our efforts to live the life He has called us to live. God does thank us through the blessings in our lives. However, we are the ones who are indebted. We are the ones who need to say, "Thank You". "Thank You, God"!

GOD DIDN'T GIVE US CREATIVE MINDS TO SEE THINGS AS THEY ARE

RATHER AS THEY CAN BE

TRUST AND HAVE FAITH

Only God Knows Where He
Wants You to Be

Only God Knows How to Get You There

Only God Gives You Every
Conceivable Thing
Required to Get You There

Do What It Is That It Is for You to Do

Then

Trust and Have Faith

INVENTORS

Inventors are visionaries. Not so much because of the ideas themselves, but in the resulting usefulness and application of what is being created. The motivation is oftentimes the result of an inventor seeking a better way to do something that they themselves cannot do or at least wish to improve upon being able to do. It is all about how the relative application of the creation, the "Tool," whether mechanical or otherwise, fulfills the purpose and desire for which it was created.

Isn't that what people are all about? God never made a car, built a house or building, anything mechanical or materialistic without the tool. He created and invented man and the animals that roam the earth. Rather interesting, God invented the inventor, the very "Tool" He needed to do the things He had the desire to create upon this earth. Yes, God created all the things that a man needs to invent and make things, but as a man can't build a house of wood without a saw and hammer, the tools, God can't build things on this earth without His tool, man.

God has provided man with the ability to develop many types of tools. Books are one type that man uses to inform, educate, inspire, and entertain themselves. Millions of books have been authored over time. The list of subjects and the intended objective of their content is immense. One would be hard pressed to find a subject that hasn't been written about and published in a book, pamphlet, or some other source, which in today's world includes electronic devices. Certainly, books have become tools by which man widens the scope of understanding, knowledge, and self-guidance.

Of all the tools God has endowed man with, the Holy Spirit is the most significant. "Awakening the Power of the Holy Spirit Within" is a "Tool" by which a person is able to improve their relationship with God and live a fulfilling life of love and peace. Even when one has turned away from God, seeking God's guidance to raise them to their highest level will renew that relationship through the "Tool", the "Holy Spirit" with which God has gifted every person. God is the Master Inventor. He provided man with everything needed to fulfill the plan He has for one's life. Nothing was overlooked or left out.

A craftsman knows the importance of maintaining the tools of his or her trade in excellent working condition in order to complete tasks successfully. Likewise, if one is to realize a working and fulfilling relationship with God, the "Tool" (the "Holy Spirit") needs to be "Awakened", nurtured, and maintained. If one phrase, one analogy, one thought-provoking idea, herein, encourages a person to improve their relationship with God through "The Awakened Power of the Holy Spirit Within", then every effort and thought has become a tool guided by God for that very purpose.

INSTRUCTIONS

It's interesting to note that many things no longer come with comprehensive instructions for learning and using them, particularly electronic devices, such as computers and smart phones.

Apparently, many of these devices have become so commonplace that it's just assumed that everyone knows every aspect of using them and how to gain the full potential they are designed for and able to provide. This is particularly true of the younger generation. For the rest, there is either the trial and error method (time consuming and frustrating) or that of seeking other sources to obtain instructions or advice. In time, without continued use and application, what was once thought to be a useful device is no longer used, set aside, and of no support at all.

In our spiritual life, we sometimes fall into the same pitfall of not having or even seeking the support beneficial to taking full advantage of the blessings God has bestowed upon each of us. Yet there are many sources available that are able to deepen our spirituality and relationship with God. Simple prayer, on a regular basis, opens the door to the awareness of God's love for us. Meditation allows for a more in-depth means of communication, not only with God, but with a person's inner source of knowledge and self-worth. Many individuals reference, and study, the Bible or read inspirational and motivational articles, periodicals, and books. Attending a group or gathering of likeminded individuals, on a regular basis, provides pier support and opens new opportunities for learning and providing a foundation upon which to build a sound relationship with God.

Like the providers of those electronic devices that require that a person seek outside sources to gain the full benefit from them, spirituality, in and of itself, cannot provide the full benefit God has intended that we gain from it. In the same way we use resources to learn to appreciate a device, spirituality can only be fully appreciated when we open our hearts and minds to the sources God has made available to us in order to strengthen and deepen our relationship, and faith, in God, the Holy Spirit within.

G–P–S

Even though we sometimes take wrong turns in life and get hopelessly lost————

God's—**P**erfect—**S**ystem

Is able to get us back on the right road in life.

If we release ourselves to God, His G-P-S will guide us in making the right turns, in the right direction, at the right time. We'll make the right decisions and the results will amaze us.

So many of us live by the concept "It's my way or the highway".

But with God, it's either a rough road that we follow on your own, or a well laid-out path of serendipitous events directed and provided by God.

OVEN

Mix all the ingredients and nothing happens, but after putting it in the oven, it becomes something.

The oven is the essential entity in order to successfully finish many recipes that require baking. To make a cake, for example, a person gathers together the varied ingredients required to put together everything necessary to make a certain type of cake. The flour, eggs, oil, flavoring, and whatever else. Then by adding the ingredients in the proper order and mixing them accordingly, it all comes together in a well-prepared substance that looks right, smells delicious, and appears to be ready to result in the perfect cake the preparer set out with the objective to achieve.

In order to finalize the process to assure the desired results however, the substance must be placed in the oven, at the proper temperature, for the necessary amount of time. One may be tempted to taste the mixture to test it. In some cases, such as with cookie dough, one might be tempted to eat some, if not all of the ingredients. However, without having completed the process by baking in the oven, some of the ingredients could be harmful an even cause illness. Likewise, if left unbaked, certain ingredients could spoil, resulting in having to discard all the ingredients and ending up with nothing.

See any parallels in the things we do in life that are similar to this? A person may embark on some type of project, which could be in connection with their job, education, household, hobby, sports and exercise, or even spiritual growth. Everything believed to be needed to complete the project can be acquired or arranged for, a time schedule can be established, and the project can begin to be put into action.

The oven? O' yes the oven, well . . . that's God. Turning the entire project over to God is like putting the ingredients for a cake into the oven. You can't see what the ingredients are doing while in the oven, but you have faith that it will turn out just the way you intended. So also with your project. Having done all that appears to be necessary to attain satisfactory results, then turning it over to the will of God and asking His guidance and blessing upon it will assure that the final results will be pleasing and rewarding. God knows how to blend the ingredients, how to portion each aspect of the project, how to hold back on some and add to others, even how to add ingredients that may have inadvertently been left out. Then God, with His perfect timing, knows exactly how long and at what intensity the efforts one needs to be put forth in order to achieve positive results.

Without turning the project over to God, one may still have a project that appears to be satisfactory. Like eating cookie dough, you may accept the unfinished project at the stage it is and settle with the results it produces. But why take the chance that it may turn bad and become a complete failure? Turning the project and your life over to God, you will be assured of achieving not only the perfect results, but results that will enable you to not only please God but glorify God. Amen!

STRANGERS

Focused on the Spirit of God within, we are aligned with the power of God working in our lives, bringing into our lives and across our path the right people, with the right gifts at the right time. It may be a family member, a friend, and oftentimes a total stranger. I was blessed to be a part of one such experience.

It was a beautiful morning, and as I was driving to the Physical Fitness Facility where I work out three days each week, my vehicle developed a weird rumbling sound. After a few miles the noise faded out and everything appeared normal. Continuing to my destination I gave little thought to there being anything significantly wrong with the vehicle. However, I recall saying to myself at the time, "If there is a problem, God, I know you will guide me through with a right outcome". Pulling up to a parking spot in front of the facility, I shut the engine off. Just to be certain everything was okay, I turned the key to restart the vehicle, and nothing, just a click.

Thinking it may just be the battery, I rationalized, if I just go in and do my routine workout, by the time I come back out the battery would regain enough strength to start the vehicle. Otherwise, I'd just have to call road service and proceed from there.

Shortly into my routine, looking out, I noticed a vehicle pull in and park next to another vehicle in the adjoining spot to where I had parked. As I watched the driver of this newly arrived vehicle lifting the hoods of both cars and getting out jumper cables, I immediately gathered my belongings and headed out.

I asked the man if he would be kind enough to also give a jump to start to my vehicle, and he responded in a friendly and positive way. Having difficulty getting results with the jumper cables he was using to start the other man's car, I offered a set of much heavier duty cables I carry at all times. With these cables the vehicle he was attempting to get started turned over immediately, and that person was soon on his way.

Turning to my vehicle and hooking up the jumper cables, nothing, still just a click. After trying a few things, it was obvious that the battery was strong and the problem was likely with the starter, so I put the cables away. Since my vehicle was a standard shift, the man offered to see if we could push it out of the parking spot and push it to see if I could release the clutch and, with the vehicle in gear, get it to start. With the man pushing and me in the driver's seat, by the grace of God, in just a few feet I was able to release the clutch and the engine started right up. Now as long as the engine kept running, I could drive to someplace to get the mechanical help I needed. I thanked the man, gave him a big hug, and wished God's blessings upon him.

This man, a total stranger, coming to the area to help another person who was also a total stranger to me, was not a coincidence. It was a matter of having faith that God would direct me to a right outcome. One that I couldn't have imagined would take place. Yet a perfect solution in a difficult situation. But God wasn't done just yet.

After going to several service centers, each one advising me that it would be a few days before they could get me in, I drove to a nearby town and to a center where I had work done on the vehicle in the past. Being advised by them that it would also be a few days before they could service the vehicle, I decided to drive home and decide how to proceed.

One consideration had to do with getting a friend, who incidentally lived in the next state and some fifty miles distance, to pick me up if I did drop off the vehicle at this or some other center. My friend had told me that this was the day she was going to travel to spend time with her sister who lived several miles away in the opposite direction. Deciding to call her anyway, I was surprised when she answered and said that for one reason or other she had decided not to go to her sister's place. In fact, she had considered traveling to the area where I lived to take care of some business matters.

A couple of hours later (in the meantime leaving my vehicle running), I drove to the familiar center, my friend arrived, and I was assured that the center would attend to my vehicle as soon as they were able to fit it in their very busy schedule.

Thinking I would be without my vehicle for a few days, I was amazed when the very next day I received a call that my vehicle had been repaired and was ready to be picked up. Additionally, I was amazed that the amount due was somewhat less than I had figured it would likely cost to have it repaired.

No, God wasn't leaving any loose ends to be taken care of. There were many little details that unfolded through this whole experience that truly demonstrated God's presence. The most significant was that God brought the right people, with the right gifts, at the right time into my life. Focused on the Spirit of God within, it becomes evident that when one is aligned with the power of God, He is proactively working in our lives.

Ps: It can't be overlooked in this day of racial tension and animosity, particularly among some younger people, the man who helped me was likely in his fifties. The man he was helping was likely in his twenties. Both were men of color. I am an elderly white man. We were simply children of God and brothers.

Pps: It is also significant to consider, while oftentimes situations cause stress, tension, call for immediate action, and may even prompt radical behavior, it is important to step back and allow the perfect unfolding of divine order to take place.

ACCOMPLISH MORE

Are our prayers answered? Absolutely! Perhaps not in the way we had asked or hoped for, but in a way that provides the highest good in our lives and in the lives of those we hold in our prayers. If we're aligned with and in relationship with God, certain prayers will not only be answered in accordance with our wishes, but in ways that go far beyond our request and fondest desires. In other words, with and through God, we'll "Accomplish More"!

There will be other times that our prayer requests will be answered in a way far less or perhaps even in a totally different way in which we had sought. However, an all knowing and loving God will fulfill our prayer requests in ways that will allow us and those we pray for to fulfill God's plan for our lives. Again, though we may be dismayed by the timing or actual way in which our prayers are answered, we will "Accomplish More"!

Through prayer and our relationship with God, as we "Awaken the Power of the Holy Spirit Within", our wishes, dreams, desires, and every need will be fulfilled and met in a timely way. Even more significantly, the answer to our prayer will prove to be an even greater blessing than we would ever have imagined or asked for. Through God's supernatural gifts and powers within we will "Accomplish More"!

"Now all glory to God, who is able, through His almighty power at work within us, to accomplish infinitely more than we might ask or think". Ephesians 3:30 (NLT)

GRACE

What is "Grace", or more specifically "the Grace of God", and what does it really have to do with one's spirituality or their relationship with God? According to one definition in Webster's dictionary, "Grace" is "unmerited divine assistance".

The word "Grace" appears 124 times in the Bible (NIV). The phrase "Grace of God", or a direct reference to "God's Grace upon man", appears 41 times. It only appears once in the Old Testament, in the Psalms. "You are the most excellent *of* men and your lips have been anointed with **grace,** since **God** has blessed you forever". *Psalm 45:2 (NIV)* It appears 40 times in the New Testament, i.e.: "but by the **Grace of God,** I am what I am". *1 Corinthians 15:10 (NIV).*

We hear the word "Grace" used in many ways in reference to how God is proactive in our lives and blesses us. "Grace" is generally thought of and used in a positive way, as something good, something to be desired. While it sometimes is associated with acknowledgment or reward, i.e.: Psalm 45:2 (NIV), "Grace" is generally referred to as a gift, unanticipated and requested, an "unmerited" gift from God.

It can be said, therefore, that one may experience the "Grace of God" as a way in which God recognizes one's good deeds or intentions. Otherwise, how does one receive, activate, or initiate the "Divine Assistance" of the "Grace of God"? Very simply, through "Faith"! Acknowledging that God is, just as He said "I AM", then have "Faith". It is through Faith that we release and activate the Grace of God in our lives! "Without Faith it impossible to please God, because anyone who comes to Him must believe that He exists and that He rewards those who earnestly seek Him" *Hebrews 11:6 (NIV).*

Many substances in our world are inert, unable to do anything on their own, even though they are designed for a specific and oftentimes, significant task. Certain types of adhesives and epoxies have co-reactants where two additives must be combined for the product to work properly. Likewise, the "Grace of God" can be much like one of these inert substances. It's there, and its purpose is to fulfill a pertinent task in our lives, but without the co-additive "Faith", Grace will remain inert.

As a person's relationship with God grows deeper and their "Faith" becomes stronger and more trusting in God's role in their life, the "Grace of God" is activated, and a person is more aware of the blessings that take place in their life. Difficult obstacles are met with confidence and quickly overcome. Doubts and fears fade and are replaced with assertiveness and a positive mind-set. The "Grace of God" implements the joy, fulfillment, love, and peace that God intends our lives to be filled with.

With "Faith," and the "Grace of God", co-additives combined and working together, God is proactive in providing His divine assistance in our lives through the ways in which He showers His blessing upon us.

Webster: Grace: unmerited divine assistance given humans for their
                   regeneration or sanctification
                   a virtue coming from God
                   a state of sanctification

STOP AND GO

Typically, when driving a vehicle, once a driver starts the engine, puts the vehicle in gear, and commences to drive to their desired destination, they leave the engine running. That is, unless they have cause to stop for an extended period of time along the way. When one has a reason to make a short stop, say for other traffic or a traffic signal, the driver brakes, comes to a stop, and the engine remains running ready to move the vehicle as the driver releases the brake and depresses the accelerator to advance accordingly. In other words, it allows the driver to "Stop and Go" as desired.

There are certain automobiles today that are considered by some to be more technically advanced because of certain features they may have. One such feature, designed to contribute to better gasoline mileage, may be referred to as "Stop, Shut Off, Turn on and Go". What it does is automatically shuts off the vehicle's engine when it comes to a stop. As a driver applies the brakes and the vehicle comes to a stop, say at a traffic signal, the engine automatically shuts off. When the driver releases the brake and depresses the accelerator to commence moving, the engine automatically starts up and the vehicle moves accordingly.

God is more traditional. God doesn't take breaks. When a person slows down and comes to a stop in their life experiences, God isn't a "Stop, Shut Off, Turn on and Go" God. Even when one's life shuts down like the technically advanced automobile waiting for you to press the go button, the accelerator, God doesn't shut down. God is always there and running prepared to move you from that position of standing still to advancing along the road of life to the destination God has set out for you to arrive at.

Your life may be at a stop, and you may not know whether to continue straight ahead in the direction you've been going, or change direction and go one way or the other. But God is still there with you. Turning to Him will give you the confidence that whichever direction you take, He will be there for the entire trip. In fact, God knows what direction His plan is for you to take, and He will guide you in making the right choice.

Some cars that are less advanced than those that shut off the engine when you come to a stop operate so quietly that when they are stopped, you can't hear the engine or tell if it is running. Likewise, you may not see or hear the way God is working in your life. God may be establishing the things necessary for you to fulfill His plan for your life without you realizing it. When it's time to move on, God will have prepared everything to fulfill every need to complete the journey.

Of course, there are also those vehicles that intentionally rumble when idling, indicating power and preparedness to make a speedily aggressive move forward. While God is generally there quietly prepared to get you going, there are times He has to be more aggressive in our lives. He has to shake us up, make some noise in our life, and rumble a little to get us going.

Regardless of what it is we need to get moving, God knows what it is that will get us back and going again. Don't shut God off. Like the engine of your car that you keep running efficiently through providing petroleum and proper service, keep God running in your life through providing the petroleum of prayer and proper service through being His instrument of love and peace.

SELF-WORTH

Many people believe and have faith in God. The fact is however, it is equally important to have faith in ourselves. Having faith in God and in ourselves is a gift, a gift from God. When we lack self-worth and fail to believe in ourselves, we are in effect, turning our back on God. We're failing to acknowledge that it is God who has given and instilled in each of us the skills, talents, and abilities we have.

We need to recognize those gifts, no matter what they are, and acknowledge that they are God-given. Every talent, skill, and ability is specifically given to us by God as a special gift in order to fulfill the specific purpose and direction God intended and has for our lives. We all have different attributes and abilities in order to achieve what it is that it is for us to do as we live out and fulfill our role upon this earth.

Isn't it a little difficult to say, "I believe in God", then somehow justify saying, "Why is God denying me the things I want and need"? Actually, we may be saying, "I know better than God what I need in my life to be happy or successful". Or, is it in fact not what we think we need to do God's will for our life, but is it greed, jealously, arrogance, and/or revengefulness that is motivating our desires. When we allow the opinion of others to have an influence on how we look at ourselves, we sometimes compare ourselves to others according to the gifts we perceive they have been given, rather than considering our own God-given uniqueness.

When one is free of the opinions of man and focuses on the gifts they do have, asking God to guide them in using those gifts to serve His purpose for their life, they will soon come to the realization and understanding that not only are they experiencing a rebirth of their faith in themselves and their abilities and potential, but they have a renewed faith and relationship with God.

"And we know that God causes everything to work together for the good of those who love God and *are called according to His purpose for the*". *Romans 8:28 (NLT)*

CONNECT THE DOTS

A basic exercise in demonstrating creativity is "Connecting the Dots". Starting with a sheet covered with dots equally and systematically placed, one can create an outline of nearly anything. As a teaching tool for children, it can be fascinating to see how their minds fabricate their idea of how something looks to them. Ask them to create a picture of a person, dog, car, house, or nearly anything, and the resulting outlines can be varied, and an interesting perspective on how different their opinions can be.

As people grow older the variations will likely become fewer and fewer. A stick person drawn by two or more people will likely look nearly identical. Except for size, a dog, car, and house will bear numerous similarities when drawn by different people. Lines between the dots will generally be drawn more readily and deliberately. Less thought will be given to individualism, and a general standard or expectation will be demonstrated.

Randomly removing dots will cause one to contemplate the various options available in order to create their vision of how something should look using the available dots. In other words, one will have to become more creative to express their thoughts and opinions as to how a certain thing should look to be recognized for what it is, or at least what it is supposed to represent. Although at times, others will never guess what it is that the person is attempting to illustrate.

Sometimes, perhaps our lives are filled with too many dots. Or, perhaps the dots in our lives are placed in such a way by others that we draw conclusions others have the desire for us to draw in order that the results will agree with the dot placer. Unfortunately, this may cause one to take the path of least resistance. Rather than using their God-given creativity to draw conclusions that fit into their parameter of dots, they are guided by someone else's.

God provides each of us with a full page, life if you will, of dots. That is how God intended for humans to interact in the world in which they exist. We are able to create anything we wish with God's supernatural gifts and wisdom. Anything our creativity is able to imagine, God gives us the ability, courage, enthusiasm, and stamina to make happen. Most importantly is the ability to think for ourselves. To ask ourselves, "Does it make sense"? Do the lines between the dots create a believable representation of what we are led to believe they are intended to represent.

Sometimes there are certain lines that can't be drawn. We may want to connect certain dots to fit the prospective we believe to be appropriate, but there is just no way to make it happen. That may be considered a time for "Having Faith", believing in God, having faith in God, appreciating that God is in control. That is a time for letting go and letting God fill in the blanks. What we may have created with our lines, even if all the dots were available to us, would be far less fulfilling and rewarding than what God is able to create.

God sees all the dots, knows all the lines that are possible to be drawn. More importantly, our loving God wants to bless us in ways in which we could never imagine possible, if we release ourselves to His will for our lives. Trusting and having faith in God allows us to be free of the expectations and opinions of others and of having to place the lines between the dots they determine we need to follow. We are all individuals with unique abilities, talents, and levels of creativity. Relying on God to guide our thinking and creativity will result in divine outcomes and clear outlines of the life and world in which we live.

ACCEPT EVIL

Generally speaking, it is not common for human nature to be evil or for people to approve of or encourage evil. At the same time, it does exist in many forms and in many ways in the world and even in our own lives. Mankind has been given the freedom by God to choose to be a part of it or reject it. In order to reject evil, it must be acknowledged and recognized for what it is. It doesn't matter the source. What does matter is realizing that we can encounter evil in the world we live in and are exposed to, as well as in our own minds, our tyrannical minds. Then, "Accepting Evil" in as much as it does exist and we are exposed to it, we are able to confront evil and overcome it and defeat it. Ignoring evil or failing to realize it is everywhere present leaves us susceptible to being overcome by the tyranny of it. It can lead us in directions that will have negative or destructive consequences in our lives. Evil can destroy relationships, health, finances, welfare, and worst of all our relationship with God.

A gardener or homeowner soon learns that ignoring the weeds in a garden or lawn will lead to the weeds taking over and eventually smothering the good and desirable plants and grass, killing everything completely. Garden plants will cease to produce healthy blossoms and beautiful flowers. Vegetable plants will be strangled by the weeds and fail to mature and produce the succulent produce one anticipates will be forthcoming. Homeowners will soon discover that the flush vibrant grass is just gangly and unsightly weeds detracting from an otherwise beautiful landscape. Hours and many dollars are spent by both gardeners and homeowners to eradicate weeds, and the battle is never ending. Even with the most effective chemicals and methods, weeds keep coming back. Year after year the vigilant and responsible gardener and homeowner devotes money and time to preserving and developing healthy and productive gardens, lawns, and other vegetation.

Evil is no different. We have the ability and the resources to overcome and defeat evil. God gives us the gifts of wisdom, discernment, willpower, self-control, and spiritual guidance to avoid being overtaken by evil. When the threats of evil to influence our lives become recognized, when we "Accept Evil" as being a threat to us, we are able to meet it head-on and defeat it. Calling upon God to provide the determination and strength through "Awakening the Power of the Holy Spirit Within", God will activate, not just the ability, but the desire to move beyond the threat evil imposes and be a conqueror and not a victim. Peace, love, and joy are the rewards, not worry, fear, and hatred. There is no obstacle that evil can pose to us in our lives that God isn't able and willing to help us challenge and overcome.

Yes, the world and even our own tyrannical minds will expose us to evil. Like the weeds of one type or another which come back time after time and year after year, evil of one type or the other will continue to try to influence our lives and actions. Recognizing it, accepting it for what it is, seeking the spiritual guidance of a loving God to curtail it, our lives will flourish like the bountiful harvest of a garden and reflect the beauty of a meticulously maintained landscape.

ASKING WHY
(Lock & Key)

God allows us to experience situations in order that He might use them in a way to fulfill His plan for our lives. Though we may ask why and question certain things, it is important to understand and accept that God has a clear intention as to why and how to use every situation to bring fulfillment and betterment into our lives.

Trusting in God's plan for our lives gives us the assuredness that nothing will go on forever. Difficult times will lead to experiences of achievement and victory. Experiences of accomplishment that we find satisfying will fade from time from time and become less rewarding.

The *key* is accepting that whatever the present situation may be, or a person is experiencing, it will change. The *lock* the key will open is the storehouse of blessings God holds for each person. Having faith that every blessing contained therein is for your good while fulfilling God's plan for your life, will lead to understanding, fulfillment, and peacefulness.

Certainly, we all have dreams and expectations for ourselves and our future. The blessings bestowed upon us by God, with which we are able to fulfill those dreams and expectations, lie in whether or not they are aligned with the plan God has for our lives. When in doubt, by releasing ourselves and our situation to God's guidance and by placing our faith in God, we will be more likely to be less subject to the opinion and influence of man and the desire for earthly possessions.

God provides absolutely everything we are in need of to fulfill His plan for our lives. If we're complaining that we lack what is needed to fulfill our plans and dreams, perhaps those plans and dreams aren't aligned with God's plan. Having faith in God's plan and committing ourselves to live by His plan to the best of our ability, will in time, prove that God's plan is a better plan, more rewarding, fulfilling, and abounds with His love and peace.

Rather than "Asking Why", consider, "How are these experiences helping me to serve and glorify God and fulfill His plan for my life"?

SCREECHING TIRES

If you've ever been in an auto accident, you would likely recognize and be familiar with the sound of screeching tires. Inevitably, the sound is followed by the menacing sound of a crash.

When we're in a troubling situation of any type, that's what our tyrannical mind does, it sets us up for the screeching tire sound scenario. In our mind we anticipate the impact and crash. In a split second, every conceivable thing that can go wrong will come to mind and try to convince us that disaster is at hand. It's like when we feel that inner small voice, gentle nudge, or unsettled feeling inside warning us that something we're doing, or about to do or be involved with isn't quite right.

While the tyrannical mind may cause us to totally overreact, we are still inclined to brace ourselves, look about, and try to anticipate a sudden impact. The screeching tires we hear, and perhaps the apparent crash we anticipate, may not even have anything to do with us. It might just be what is happening somewhere around us and to others. We may hear, or even be close enough, to see vehicles slamming into one another, while we ourselves are guided free and safe of any impending crash or disaster.

The same occurs with the warning signs that are pertinent to what we're about to do in our personal lives and where we're headed. It may be a signal to look at the situation in order to make a reassessment of it all. Then again, the feelings about a personal challenge or problem may not have to do with a situation involving one's self, but rather something impacting another person's life, perhaps a relative or someone we're close to and care about. The situation may not affect us in any personal way, but we are alerted to the need to show understanding, compassion, and offer prayer.

Whether it's an actual incident in the street, neighborhood, city, or elsewhere, or a personal situation that the inner feeling warns us about, with the Holly Spirit guiding us, we will be led in a direction and path of safety that leads us to our highest good.

EXPECTING TOO MUCH

Traveling anywhere, to work, to the store, or on a local or cross-country trip, we rely on signage to help us get to where we're going. Without signs, maps, and directional devices, we would lose our way, encounter mishaps, and perhaps never reach our destination.

Then why doesn't God provide us with more obvious signage, directions, and other divine devices to assist us in reaching our spiritual destination? Is God "Expecting Too Much"?

Certain religions advocate that writings contained in books (i.e., the Bible, the Book of Mormon, the Qur'an, and others) contain all the guidance we need if we read them and follow their teachings. Yet to some, they seem to be vague and certainly not as direct as looking at a road sign with specific directions as to the way we need to go to get to our destination.

Is God "Expecting Too Much"? The revelation and answer to this question is in one simple yet awesome word, "Faith". When we have faith in God, and in fact in ourselves in trusting that God has blessed us with all we need to fulfill His plan for our lives, faith assures us that God will keep us on the right path to reach our spiritual destiny. God only asks and expects us to believe in Him and have faith in Him and His love for us.

Is that "Expecting Too Much"?

CONUNDRUM

According to Wikipedia, Conundrum may refer to: A logical postulation[1] that evades resolution, an intricate and difficult problem.

There are times we need blinders on, looking straight ahead, having faith in where we're headed, trusting that we're being guided by God and following the direction He intends for us to take.

Other times we need to slow down, open our eyes wide to all that is around us and perceive the glory of the amazing path we are being directed by God to follow.

So, what is it, blinders or expanding our view? An intricate and difficult problem! A conundrum? Perhaps we need to do both!

At times it is important to avoid the distractions of the world around us. Refusing to be tempted by the greed, jealousy, and arrogance that influences us to want to grab for more. Resisting being pulled in by "Political Correctness", the hype of social media, news on television and in print. Concentrating instead on what is ours to do, while not being concerned about the opinion of others or trying to keep up or outdo those we associate with.

At other times, however, it may be important to be aware of those things that may have an impact and a positive or otherwise adverse effect on our daily lives. The way in which we respond and react to situations and events, may have a negative effect on how we think and how we are affected by things we may or may not have control over. It may be to our advantage to listen and consider the opinions of others. We may find new interests we here-to-for were not aware of and learn new and better approaches to dealing with common challenges.

God did not intend for us to isolate ourselves from the world around us. Rather, God has given us insight and wisdom to be discerning in what to avoid and what to be cognizant of, in order to take advantage of, and bring joy, fulfillment, and blessings into our lives. When we're in relationship with God, what otherwise may be a conundrum becomes a logical postulation with resolution.

[1]*Postulation: to assume or claim as true, existent, or necessary.*

PEANUT BUTTER

Take a bunch of peanuts,
remove them from their shell,
crush them all up,
add a few ingredients to make them into a smooth mixture, and

OUT COMES PEANUT BUTTER!

You probably never gave it a thought that God can do exactly the same thing with our lives.

Take a bunch of times we've been a nut job and remove that protective shell we've placed around ourselves to hide all our past indiscretions. Then break it all down by crushing all the evil allowed to take place and add a few ingredients, such as God's love, compassion, healing, and holiness. Then combine it with God's desire and ability to smooth out one's life by setting aside the things of the past, and OUT COMES A RENEWED CHILD OF GOD!

Well, comparing it to peanut butter may be a stretch.

When we turn to God, counsel with God the many times we've allowed our tyrannical mind to lead us astray and commit indiscretions against God, our neighbor, and even ourselves, we can be assured that God will "Set Aside the Things of the Past". By doing so, God will guide us along new paths. God will give us direction, strength, and supernatural abilities to change our lives and fulfill the purpose God has for our lives.

God has prepared and willed each of us to be instruments of love and peace. Through much of our lives we may take a detoured lifestyle that is far from representing the plan God has for us and provided for us to take. No matter how far we may have strayed, once we turn back to God's loving concern for us, God will use every life experience and the situations we've encountered, good and bad, and use them to His advantage. That is when, as a renewed child of God, we will truly be the instrument of love and peace that God intended for us to be.

MY FILING CABINET

As our lives unfold, we begin to record the events of our lives and place them in files similar to expandable folders which we file away in cabinets. We develop a folder of good things (BLESSINGS) and a folder of things that are negative or undesirable (THE BAD THINGS).

The blessings are the things, small and great, that our higher power (God) brings into our lives and we openly accept, embrace, recognize, and thank God for. That not only includes our faith, love of another, health, well-being, friends, and other people, it includes the feelings, experiences, places, and circumstances that bring happiness and joy into our lives and give us fulfillment, contentment, and peaceful feelings. For a blessing to go into the folder, we must recognize it as such and be thankful for it and recognize the good it has contributed to our life. This file grows very slowly for many people. Oftentimes, it hardly fills even a small expandable folder, particularly through most of one's early years.

On the other hand, "The BAD THINGS" folder seems to begin to fill rapidly as life comes at us fast. We tend to experience influences that begin to affect us negatively. We become judgmental of others and particularly of ourselves and of the things we think, say, and do. We allow our peers to be our judge and influence the way we live, or should live our lives. We begin to take blame for circumstances around us we may have no control over. We allow negativism to creep in and begin to look at the cup as being half empty rather than half full. We think of all the reasons that something can't be done rather than looking at the rewards of pursuing challenges.

The result, the small file folder of "THE BAD THINGS" gives away to a single drawer file cabinet, then two drawers, four drawers, multiple four drawer cabinets, etc. We accumulate large files of things that negatively impact our lives and, in most cases, keep us from being all that God had set us in this place in the world to be.

In the meantime, the "BLESSINGS" folder remains small and rather insignificant. A file that could easily sit atop the row of four drawer files holding all "THE BAD THINGS."

Fortunately for many, there comes a time in our lives when we begin to realize how fortunate we are, how much good has happened in our lives, and gradually we acknowledge that our higher power (God) has truly been good to us and blessed us. The more we recognize how our lives have been impacted by a loving, healing, forgiving, restoring God, the fuller that our "BLESSINGS" folder becomes. Not long after, that small folder gives away to a single drawer file cabinet, then a two-drawer, four-drawer, and multiple four-drawer cabinets, which become filled to overflowing capacity and requires more and more space in which to be stored.

This awakening stirs the awareness that all those experiences and influences that had affected us negatively in the past are perhaps no longer as significant. One by one these items filed away in "THE BAD THINGS" files lose their power and significance, through and by our accepting the forgiveness of God, as we begin to forgive ourselves. We let go of the past and begin to release negativism, guilt, remorse, disappointment, fear, rejection, all the things that have held us back, suppressed ambitions and feelings.

What God wants is for all "THE BAD THINGS" files to be emptied and thrown out, cast aside, and never rekindled in our lives or even our thoughts. Concentrating instead on the "BLESSINGS" folders. Be thankful that we are in the hands of a caring, giving, and watchful God whose intentions are for us to live happy, peaceful, and fulfilling lives.

BELIEVING VS. KNOWING

To believe something
leaves room for doubt and uncertainty

"I believe a certain thing to be true or real".
Because, as far as I know, it is true.

To know something
represents a fact, an absolute

"I know it is real, exists, or is in fact true".
Because, I have seen it, experienced it.

OUTSPOKEN OR CONSISTENT

It's Not So Important to Be Outspoken
in Attempting to Accomplish Making
Changes in This World

As It Is

To Be Consistent
in Making Changes in a Way That They
Will Show God
Our Appreciation
for the Gifts He Has Given Us
and in the Ways We Use Them

OUR WAY—GOD'S WAY

As long as a person keeps on insisting on doing it their way, they are preventing God from doing it His way. They are limiting themselves to a narrow path with blinders on. They must learn to let go and let the all-knowing, all-able, all-giving God direct their path. God's desire is to bless and provide in ways well beyond our own ability to imagine or achieve.

When we strive while devoting time and energy to a project or quest, be it materialistic, a relationship or whatever, yet we never appear to be making any progress towards achieving whatever it is, it's important to ask, are we insisting on doing it "Our Way"? Is God failing to answer our desires because He has a better plan, a better path through which we can fulfill His plan for our life.

Before we were even born, God had a plan for our lives. God gave every one of us everything we could conceivably need to carry out His plan. We were also blessed with a free will. A will to determine if we are going to seek God's guidance in using the gifts He blessed us with to fulfill His plan or turn away from God and insist on doing it "Our Way".

It is very likely that doing it "Our Way" rather than "God's Way" will lead to many dead-ends and disappointments. That does not mean that doing it God's way will never present challenges and times that we will have to reassess where we are and the path we're taking. At times like this, God is always there to guide us, to redirect our path if necessary, and in some way assure us that in the end we are going to be exactly where we are supposed to be.

Following God's way may very likely be difficult at times. Knowing that we are continually being counseled by God, who is keeping an eye upon us, helps us through those times and gives us the perseverance to keep moving forward with confidence, while enthusiastic and at peace as the journey unfolds. God's plan is for us to enjoy life and take advantage of every opportunity to explore the wonders of His creation, this world and everything upon it. God has given us the gifts and the opportunity in order to do this to the full extent, doing it "God's Way"! Will "Your Way" provide the same awesome opportunities?

It is never too late to turn to God and boldly declare, "God, my way just isn't resulting in the things I had anticipated would happen, if I kept pursuing them". Please God, accept my desire and willingness to release my life to You and follow Your plan. Guide me in every aspect of my life and use the gifts You have blessed me with to glorify You in all that I do. Praise you, God, and thank you for being a God who sets aside the things of the past and re-charts the path of my life that I might fulfill Your plan."

APPROACHING GOD

The way in which a person approaches God is very significant. Approaching God humbly with "Cup in Hand" is the way many people turn to God. Another way is with "Boldness", a direct approach acknowledging one's indiscretions as well as blessings. Is one or the other the right way or the most appropriate way? The fact is, simply approaching God and involving Him in one's life and in life decisions is the important thing.

It may be that what God really wants is for a person to stand in His presence and "Boldly" present themselves openly and without reservation. Approaching God humbly with "Cup in Hand" may indicate shame and a desire to hide the things one is unwilling to face up to. God already knows what you've done in and with your life. God is the one who is best able to determine if what a person has done is wrong. God is the only one who sees and knows that what in the eyes of man is shameful may have implications. Isn't what God really wants us to do is stand in His presence and say, "God, I've messed up and made some horrible decisions. I've done things I'm not proud of, and in fact am ashamed of. I know the consequences I've been victimized by, and they are of my own doing." There is no room for "I Think" when standing in the presence of God, because, God knows.

When we stand "Boldly" and ask God to guide us in the future to avoid doing the things we have acknowledged are less than what God expects of us, God sets aside those things. God is not a God who condemns, but a God who has the desire to help us improve our lives. God awaits our simple prayer for the strength and fortitude to change our lives. God already is aware of what it is that we have to do to change the direction of our lives. Through the "Awakened Power of the Holy Spirit Within" we will be guided with the supernatural strength to resist old habits, relationships, and situations that led us astray in the past.

It isn't easy. The suggestive power of the tyrannical mind is very influential. It never reminds us of negative outcomes or side effects. It only induces one to think of the pleasure, be it brief, or the short-lived joy or exhilaration a certain experience or situation may provide. Then, of course, one is likely to experience the consequences of remorse with a tyrannical mind more inclined to say, "I told you so", rather than showing empathy or suggesting that it might not be a good thing to repeat. Rather, the tyrannical mind is ever ready and prepared to suggest: "Hey, do it again, I dare you!"

The amazing thing is that when we "Stand Boldly" in the presence of God and seek His guidance and supernatural gifts of strength and willpower, we are opening a dialogue with a Friend, a God who wishes to be our Companion, our Personal Life Trainer. We are establishing the way to a new relationship with God and a new life for ourselves. A life in which we will be favored by God and blessed in more ways than we could ever have previously imagined.

Be Bold, be direct, be open, it's time to face up!

YOU DON'T BELIEVE?

You don't believe in God and that He is the Creator of all things?

OBVIOUSLY

In the spring of the year you haven't looked around to see what is happening!

Everything is majestically being transformed before your very eyes! Trees that were barren are being cloaked with incredible colors of blossoms and leaves. Shoots are springing forth from the earth where their roots were nestled dormant for the winter. Flowers are blossoming with an array of intricate buds and blossoms. Birds flutter around alluring one another to mate in order to produce offspring.

How is this all possible? Does man have the ability to do any of this, or for that matter, prevent it and stop it from happening? Who could have imagined all the intricate details of it all, who could have designed it all, who could make it all happen? Is there a human being on this earth who individually, or people collectively, who have the power or ability to make any of this happen?

NO !

Therefore. . .

YES !

There is a God, a loving God, who has, is, and will continue to make it happen for all time!

Do you still choose not to believe? Perhaps you are sightless, your senses have been dulled,

and you are without emotion. Perhaps you have ceased to be a part of this awesome world.

"For His invisible attributes, namely his eternal power and divine nature, have been clearly perceived, ever since the creation of the world, in the things that have been made, so they are without excuse." Romans 1:20 (ESV)

FACE UP!

Many times in life when things don't appear to be going the way we want or expect, we tend to look around searching for someone or something to blame. We fail to consider that perhaps for one reason or another, we ourselves, because of something we have, or have not done, is the reason.

When we "Face Up", to the fact that we've messed up,

then. . .

We gain the favor of God!

In addition, and ironically,

We free ourselves of guilt!

Acknowledging our own mistakes, or even taking into account our accomplishments, frees us from restraints we otherwise place upon ourselves. Each of us has been blessed by God with the gifts of many talents, skills, and abilities—all of which God has specifically provided us with in order that we might fulfill the plan He has for our life.

Sure, we all have a plan in our mind that we think is the ideal plan to give us peace, joy, and fulfillment. Or, is it a plan to give us recognition, accomplishment, and wealth. Will our plan use those gifts in a way to glorify God, to acknowledge His love for us? God does have a plan, and it's a better plan than we could ever imagine or come up with ourselves. God's plan frees us from the "opinion of man," and allows us to be the person He created us to be.

When we "Face Up", releasing ourselves to God's will and plan for our life, everything we put our hands to do will succeed. We will experience tranquility, happiness, and accomplishment by using the gifts God blessed us with. We will have gained the favor of God.

THANK YOU, GOD,

FOR BLESSING ME

There are so many examples in my life where You have favored me, Lord, with wondrous gifts. Everyday events, friendships, skills, and accomplishments are only a few of the areas in which You have favored me and made my life fulfilling.

FOR TEACHING ME

Though I have made many mistakes and decisions that I shouldn't have made, Lord, You have used every one to your advantage, in order to teach me and help me improve and grow to become a better person.

FOR GUIDING ME

As my constant companion and ever-faithful friend, Lord, you have led me away from harm and danger. You have protected me in times of uncertainty and doubt and directed me in following the clear direction You have for my life.

STATIC – DYNAMIC

God did not provide us with the many wonderful things we share and are a part of on this earth with the intent that they should go unchanged and remain static. God gave us creative minds and an imagination in order to see things, not as they are, but as they can and could be. We must ask ourselves, "What is it that we can do to glorify God and thank Him for the precious gifts He has blessed us with, by enhancing those gifts".

As one looks around at the world and all it encompasses, it is obvious that many things in this world are beyond the ability of man to create or even duplicate in any way. That, one would assume, would only lead one to declare, "There is a God"! A God who created all things. Yet, God has blessed us with the ability to be co-creators with Him in order that we are able to make things *dynamic*. Without the God-given basics plus the materials, creativity, imagination, skills, and tools, everything would remain as it is, unchanged and *static*.

Through use, and/or neglect, things in and on this earth may be left to decay and become less useful, appealing, or beautiful. A house or building, left unused and unoccupied, may be abandoned and left to deteriorate. A vehicle left to rust or become undriveable and unused will likely end up in a junkyard. Even our own bodies and minds, without proper care or through abuse, may be allowed to deteriorate at a much younger age than intended by God. Things once dynamic, become static!

Even so, if not restorable in their entirety, in part they can be used in the revitalization of like things. Artifacts from buildings and houses may be incorporated in new architecture. Parts from worn-out vehicles are often used to replace damaged or nonfunctioning parts of others. Even human bodies can be revitalized through a changed lifestyle, diet, or pattern of exercise. Parts of a human body may be used to save or improve a life of another. Interest in the importance and advantage of recycling has become an integral part of improving our lives and the way we live.

These are ways that God provides for us to use our creative minds to see things as they can, could, and should be. That is not to indicate that God didn't make everything perfect to begin with, just as they are. However, perhaps it was God's intention in the first place, in the way He designed His creation, that through the blessings He has bestowed upon us and provided, there are yet things that could be done. Accepting things as they are allows things to remain *static* in a world in which God's plan is for things to be *dynamic*! Embellishing things God created is a way in which we thank God for giving us opportunities to be cocreative with Him.

CA-HOOTS
(noun: partnership, league)

Did you ever take into consideration that our minds and bodies are in cahoots?

How quick our bodies are to agree with our minds!

We think: It's been a hard day, I don't want to prepare dinner!

You Respond: You know, I'm not really hungry anyway (while all the time your stomach is growling asking for nourishment). Besides, I'm tired and my feet ache!

So, your mind and body agree with each other, and you snack on some ships, have some ice cream, and watch TV.

Sound familiar?

The reverse is the same. Morning has arrived, the sun is brightly shining, it's time to get up. As you start to roll out of bed, you're a little stiff, there's a little soreness in your back, and your body is saying, "I don't want to get out of bed yet"! Yep, they're in ca-hoots! The mind is right with it. I think I need another hour to let my body heal and get these kinks out. So, they agree, and two hours later you wake up and end up being late for work, school, or whatever.

Interesting how quickly we are able to be influenced by some little thought, feeling, or incident and do something we know we shouldn't, or perhaps in some cases, should be doing. And even more alarming, how at times these little things we allow to influence us, result in major consequences. True, one incident may not provoke a negative result. However, could that heart attack have been prevented had we been better stewards of our health and diet over the years? Was it our own fault that we lost that great job that we were sure would provide us with a secure future?

It only takes a small drop of water, continually dripping, to make a puddle, and as the puddle grows it become a stream, then a river that keeps pushing its banks wider and wider until it spills over its banks and becomes destructive. If we allow our minds and bodies to continue their little game of justification and permissiveness, the accumulative results are likely to lead to negative consequences, which we will suffer from greatly in the future.

It is by introducing a referee into the game, to outline the rules, and make certain that the mind and body are adhering to the rules, that this partnership can be broken up. The referee is the Holy Spirit. "Awakening the Power of the Holy Spirit Within", we will provide a realistic balance between thoughts and actions and feelings and motivation. We will have the "I can do this attitude". We may be tired, yet realize we'll probably feel much better if we do prepare a good meal and eat. It may be tempting to stay in bed every once in a while, the boss will understand, but what about that bonus at the end of the year for being a good and faithful employee.

God gave us a free will. He gave us willpower and self-motivation. These are blessings and gifts He has instilled within each of us. Because we have a free will, we can choose to use these gifts or ignore them. God also instilled with each of us "The Holy Spirit", our inner referee. It is entirely up to every one of us as to whether or not we take advantage of the gifts God has so richly blessed us with. Being in "cahoots" with God, "The Holy Spirit", those abundant blessings will enrich our lives.

RAILROAD CROSSING

Accepting God's presence in our lives is a matter of knowing God is always there to protect us from evil or any form of danger, "IF", we heed His warning and are guided by it.

It's like being at a railroad crossing when the gates have come down, the lights are flashing, and the bells are ringing. It's best to understand that danger is approaching, so we should be alert, pay attention, and respect the warning signs.

However, if we decide to ignore the warning signs and go around the railroad crossing gates and attempt to cross the railroad tracks, while we may be fortunate and avoid the disaster of being struck by the oncoming train, chances are we will be overtaken and end up in a terrible situation.

God shows His love for us by sending warning signals. God knows what will happen if we are arrogant and consider ourselves to be invincible. Therefore, God speaks to us in many different ways. It may be a little pain that alerts us to a more urgent medical problem. Perhaps an anxious feeling, about continuing to do a task we have embarked upon, will be a warning sign. It can be advice from a person we respect that helps us to see a situation more clearly.

If we fail to accept God into our lives, seeking His guidance and acknowledging God's warning signals, we may be destined for disaster. It would be like coming up to the railroad crossing without signaling devices to warn if a train is coming, ignore any impending danger, then even fail to look to see if there is a danger in crossing the tracks.

On the other hand, releasing ourselves to the mighty hand of God, keeping Him constantly in our heart, seeking His guidance, God will direct our path. God will guide us away from self-inflecting circumstances of potential danger. God has a plan laid out for every one of us. God does not want us to cut that plan short by doing foolish things and by being self-indulging in destructive ways. God's plan is for our lives is to be whole, fulfilled, joyful, loving, and peaceful.

WHITE-OUT

(The Eraser)

Perhaps not so common today with how word processing is done in the technological age we live in, as it was in the old typewriter days, White-Out was often used to delete errors. While some may have used erasers or other means of removing and reinserting words, White-Out was a popular choice for many. While it is still used today in certain situations, for those who are unfamiliar with White-Out, it was a paste-like liquid that came in a little bottle with a little brush connected to the inside of the cap. A person could use it to brush over printed or written words to hide them. Because of its quick drying properties, the person could then type or write over the hidden word or phrase correcting it.

Sometimes in our lives we do things we regret or would like to cover up in order to do over as well. Perhaps it is something we have said or done that has offended or hurt someone or even ourselves. Like the printed word on paper, we can't do anything to make it go away, what is done is done. With the grace of God, like using White-Out to cover up something in print in order to replace it and start over, the Holy Spirit of God will help us to set aside the things of the past in order to start over. One might say, "A loving and compassionate God is our White-Out of life". Using White-Out doesn't remove what has been covered up, it allows for it to be replaced with a corrected or better choice of words. Likewise, setting aside the things of the past does not mean they go away. It only means we will correct and replace them.

God is there to help us make the changes in our lives that will guide us in following the plan He called us to live by. A plan utilizing our skills, talents, and resources to find fulfillment while glorifying God through the way in which we use those blessings.

Just as assuredly as a typist will make mistakes, we also make mistakes and poor choices at times. The way we respond will result in allowing those mistakes to remain as a part of the story of our life, or we can do things that will stand out and overshadow them.

Releasing ourselves to the will of God purposefully, we will be guided in making right choices as we move forward in life. The grace of God, fulfilled in us through the Awakened Power of the Holy Spirit Within, will be our guide and our strength.

INCLUDE GOD

Many times, when we turn to God in prayer, it is in regard to asking God's help in making decisions or guiding us in what we should do, or not do, in a certain situation. Oftentimes, it is a matter that we consider could have a significant impact, positive or negative, on our lives or the life of someone close to us. It may have to do with health, finances, relationships, family, occupation, or even our spirituality. It is certainly wise to seek God's guidance in times like this. Trusting that God knows what is best for us is acknowledging that it is His plan for our lives, which we have the will and desire to follow.

What about the times we have decisions to make about things we consider may have no negative side? We seldom ask God for help and guidance in those situations. We just surge forward with what seems to be the best of the differing ways to go. We fail to give any thought as to whether one way or the other may be how God truly has the desire to raise us to our highest level in the way we serve and glorify Him. In every aspect of our lives, we will be at peace and find fulfillment if we include God in every phase of our lives, and in every decision we are faced in making, no matter how critical or consequential it may be.

God is not only our Creator, but the one who controls everything around us. We may be the ones who create situations in our lives through our decisions and actions, but God is already aware of their ramifications in our lives and the lives of others. God has already devised a plan that will fulfill His purpose for our lives. It is therefore important to make every decision, and everything you do in life, count. Relying on God, in all things, is the way in which to be sure we are being supernaturally guided to right choices that do count.

We almost instinctively turn to God in some way when things are turning against us. There are examples of a person who had turned his or her entire life against God, who in the minute of trial and without hesitation, called out to God to be merciful and spare them from utter catastrophe. The problem is, they can't be sure if the very God they are calling upon even exists, much less will do anything about their situation.

Only God knows the way to respond in a situation like this. When we believe and acknowledge God as being a loving, compassionate, all-powerful God, in good times and times of trial, an ever-present guide who watches over us when we call out, there is no doubt that our cry is heard and will be answered.

Significantly, when we seek God's presence and His hand in our moment of need, no matter the nature or significance, it will be answered in a way that is for our highest good. The road on which God leads will provide us with the way in which to find fulfillment, peace, and joy, and serve His purpose of being His instruments of love and peace. It will also please God, which will lead Him to shower favor upon our lives.

SEVEN YEARS

It is said that in a seven-year period, every single cell in a person's body is replaced with a new healthy and whole cell, replacing the old. That being the case, not just currently healthy cells, but every damaged, unhealthy, or even cancerous cell will be replaced. The problem is when new healthy cells are sometimes immediately attacked by the existing and aggressive unhealthy cells, which being dominant, maintain the sickly or diseased condition in the body.

Medical research wages an endless battle in this fight between healthy cells and those that attack organs of the body, and in some cases the entire body. Amazing strides have been made in winning this battle over time, particularly with certain diseases and medical conditions. There are, in fact, some that have been completely eradicated or at least have become controllable. That being the case however, it sometimes appears that the methods used to advance a cure can be worse than the ailment or problem itself. Nonetheless, medical advancements keep gaining ground.

There is little doubt that a person's personal attitude and mental approach to their medical condition, plays a significant role in their responding to the particular treatment and the care they may be receiving. For some, self-pity or a negative attitude contributes to the "Why Me" way in which they face the situation. For others a passive attitude results in a hopeless feeling that prevents them from expecting anything good to come of all the attention and treatment. Then there are those who take a more positive and aggressive approach. These people welcome the sincerity of those who are there to encourage and help them. Whether it be the doctors, medical staff, family members, or acquaintances, the patient makes every effort to cooperate and do the upmost to support a plan of wholeness and recovery.

People with this approach to their condition are the type that rely on the loving, healing hand of God and the power of His Holy Spirit. They are the type that pray that every new cell is supported in every way to fight off the attack of aggressive unhealthy cells. They, in fact, visualize healthy cells attacking and destroying the invasive sickly or diseased cells striving for dominance in one's body. With the aid of medical techniques and medications provided by the Health Care System, the mighty power of the Holy Spirit of God, one's faith and positive attitude, instead of taking "Seven Years" to return the body to complete health and wholeness, it may only take a few days, weeks, months, or one or two years.

In a health crisis, not every cell in the body has to be necessarily replaced immediately, only those that are deceased or unable to contribute to a healthy body. For some treatments, however, massive destruction of both good and bad cells of a certain type is necessary. Regeneration of these types of cells can be a challenge for the body and present other complications. As a person focuses on new, healthy, strong cells being created in their body, and praises God for the miracle of wholeness and healing through the Holy Spirit Within, a person's negative or passive attitude becomes one of hope, courage, trust, and positive expectations.

If you or someone you care about deeply is presently experiencing a health challenge, no matter how traumatic or significant, turn to God. Accept God's love and praise Him for the gift of life and wholeness. Feel the peace in knowing that God is with you, or the one you care about, and fighting this battle right along with you. Discomfort, pain, and suffering may linger for a while, but God, His love for you, and the healing power of His Holy Spirit Within you, will endure forever!

DEFAULT–INTENTION

There are only two ways to live our lives, by *default* or with *intention*. When we are passive and just accept life the way it is, regardless as to how life treats us, we are living by default[1] When we take an active role in decision-making in our lives, devise plans and set goals, we are living with intention[2]

The question we have to ask ourselves is; "Are we content and happy to let others make decisions for us and set the parameters[3] by which and within which we live our lives"? Are we willing to live by other's standards and expectations? There's nothing wrong with that as long as we are content, happy, and at peace with ourselves. If however, we have a tendency to feel jealous, greedy, or have a desire to be revengeful, then perhaps living by default isn't really what we want out of life or how we really want to live our lives.

The difficulty is, how do we change? We may have been at ease with the world around us, our status, and our position, until suddenly we see our lives passing before us without our having, what we are now judging, much to show for it. For certain, that is a time to turn to God and seek His plan for your life. You may consider yourself to be a Godly person having a good relationship with God. You do your best to live a good life, living resource-fully and responsibility, but are you being all that God created you to be? Have you been using the strengths God gave you with which to honor Him? Is it God who is calling you? Is it God who is challenging you to follow a new dedication, to act in a new way?

God has high expectations for each of us. The wonderful thing about God however, is the fact that He gives us everything that we could conceivably require to fulfill His plan for our lives. Seeking God's guidance will awaken the skills and talents that we may have long forgotten we had, and even more importantly, enjoyed doing and using. God knows how to light that enthusiasm within each of us that will enable us to live lives of intention.

Could it be God who actually initiated that "tendency" to feel jealous, greedy, and have a desire to be revengeful? God uses many different ways to get us to do what is ours to do.

The key word is "tendency." God does not encourage the evils of such things as jealousy, greed, or the desire to be revengeful. However, God also knows that a person who is living a life by default sooner or later may very well turn to such evils. The all-knowing God is aware of how and when to intervene and how to take action before we step over that line. Being mindful of how we are living our lives and being open to God's plan for our lives will certainly be rewarding and lead us to living lives that are fulfilling.

1 Default (Noun) Failure to do something required by duty or law A selection made usually automatically or without consideration do to the lack of a viable alternative.

A selection automatically made in the absence of choice.

2 Intention (Noun) The thing you plan to do or achieve, an aim or purpose.

Determination to act in a certain way What one intends to do or bring about

3 Parameters (Noun) A rule or limit that controls what something is or how something should be done.

Boundary or outer limits

The Higher and More Difficult the Mountain One Must Climb,

The More Rewarding and Magnificent Is the View at the Top.

TRUST, STRENGTH, COURAGE

My Faith in You, God,

When translated to

Trust, Strength, and Courage

gives me the ability

to live a life of

peace and fulfillment

knowing that I am following the clear path

God has for my life.

WHAT DOES IT MATTER?

Are you where you want to be? You may be thinking, "I wish I was on a beautiful ocean-front beach at a luxurious resort, or at some spectacular concert or special sports event, perhaps in some foreign country exploring historic architecture". You may be wishing you were hiking along an awesome trail through a forest in the mountains marveling at the wonder of nature. You may visualize walking along a seemingly endless flowing stream that cascades down an incredible ancient old waterfall and then rushes on out of sight. Don't thoughts like that sound appealing and inviting?

Fact is, "What Does It Matter", if you are aware that no matter where you are, you are in the presence of God. It is in His presence that everything becomes beautiful. Not in the surroundings where you may find yourself or even where you may want to be. It is being "Awakened to the Power of the Holy Spirit Within" that expands your senses to appreciate the things around you and where you are.

You are where you are for one of two reasons. Either God led you there by your following His plan for your life, or you were led there by the suggestions and motivation of the tyrannical mind.

If led there by God, you will experience beauty, goodness, fulfillment, and peace. If led by the tyrannical mind, you may be experiencing evil, fear, greed, jealousy, resentfulness, or tyranny.

What does it matter? If you acknowledge that you are in the presence of God, through the power of the Holy Spirit, no matter where you are, the desire to be elsewhere will be insignificant. Contrarily, if the tyrannical mind has closed out the presence of God and the Holy Spirit in your life, chances are that you have the burning desire to be somewhere else.

It is a blessing to be in a position to travel to different, interesting, and sometimes spectacular places and be a part of special experiences. For many people those opportunities do become available to them from time to time. However, one's presence at one or all of the "Worldly Wonders" or events will never be the perfect place if God and the Holy Spirit of God are not the focus of where you are, and more importantly, why you are there. God has a plan, so trust and have faith in it, "That Is What Matters"!

THE BLESSING OF THE BRAKES

I wasn't really sure if I needed the brakes on my pickup truck worked on, however something didn't sound right, like maybe a front wheel bearing may be going bad. I'm not a mechanic, and it seems like every time I try to do something on a vehicle it ends up going bad. So why I thought the noise I was hearing was the wheel bearing, I really can't say. I had checked to see if something was rubbing a tire or something else was wrong, but I couldn't see anything wrong.

Anyway, I decided to take the truck to a mechanic to have the wheel bearings checked. At the same time, I asked them to check the brakes. After all, the mileage on the truck had just gone over 100,000 miles, and I had never had anything done to the brakes previously. As I do a fair amount of driving in the mountains of the Carolinas, I figured it would be a good idea.

So the day I took the truck in, I stayed and waited for the mechanic to check it out and do the work that needed to be done. After a couple of hours, the mechanic who was working on the truck came and got me and explained that he had run into some additional problems. Taking me back to the bay where the truck was, he said that in fact the wheel bearings were very bad and about to give out, consequently he replaced them. He also showed me that the brakes were pretty bad, so he had replaced the rotor assembly on the front brakes. Then he explained, thinking the job was done and all was well, as he backed the truck out of the bay, he lost all pressure in the brakes, i.e. the brakes gave out and failed to stop the truck. He pulled it back into the bay, and upon further inspection, found that a brake line had burst and was losing all the brake fluid.

Sooooo, calling a friend to pick me up to bring me home, I left the truck for the mechanic to get the parts and repair the brake line the following day. I reasoned that it was a blessing that the brake line gave out where it did, rather than when I was driving, because it could possibly have caused an accident. The following day, when I picked the truck up, the mechanic explained that another brake line was also ready to give out, so he replaced that also. So I was good to go. I spent more than I had hoped to have to spend, however, I again reasoned that it was a blessing to have it done right. Besides, God already knew all this beforehand anyway, and He was in control and would provide.

Little did I know. . . !

The truck was driving great. Brakes were solid, no more wheel bearing noise, everything was working as one would expect, and I was certainly thankful that it was. I picked the truck up on a Thursday. The following Monday, while returning from running errands, at one point I went the opposite way from that which I would normally go. I headed down a slight slope, and stopping at a main crossroad, the angle of the cross road and overgrown bushes prevented me from clearly see oncoming traffic. However, from what I could see, it appeared the way was clear to enter the crossroad and continue on my way. Just as I started to enter the crossroad another truck crossed in front of me at a very high rate of speed. Noticing it approaching out of the corner of my eye just in time, I hit the brakes and fortunately avoided a collision with the other vehicle, which I am certain would have been catastrophic because of the speed the vehicle was moving. Praise God for the good brakes!!

It wasn't until a few days later, as I was reflecting on the incident, that I realized how God truly not only blessed me but was proactive in my life.

First: He alerted me to the potential problem with the brakes with the noise of the wheel bearing. Otherwise, I may have put it off figuring all was okay. Besides, I didn't really have the money to have the truck, much less the brakes, serviced.

Second: I was guided to a conscientious mechanic who not only knew his job and was proficient, but took the time to do it right and explain and show me what it was that needed to be done.

Third: Just a month before this all happened, I received an offer and applied for a credit card that offered no interest credit for one year. God knew I could use a little financial help in meeting this unexpected expense well before it actually occurred. Not sure how I would have been able to come up with the money otherwise to pay for the work. It allowed me to pay it over time.

Forth: God knew I would have a potential problem with the bad brake lines. He knew that if I didn't get them repaired, I could have very likely been driving down that incline, applied the brakes to stop at that crossroad, and with their failing, I would have likely coasted down into the path of that other vehicle.

Am I blessed? Is God watching over me? Is God proactive in my life?

Truly I say, "Praise God, I am blessed, I am protected, by the grace of God, and I am able to give testimony to His almighty goodness in my life."

How has God taken a proactive role in your life? Stop from time to time and reflect on God's goodness. He is watching over you! Thank and praise Him for His many blessings.

THE FIRST RESPONDER

Keep in mind
if you should ever have an emergency
and dial 911,
of all the first responders
who will come to your aid,
God will be the first one to arrive!
In fact, He'll be there the second the emergency occurs!

EVIL FOR GOOD

Innovation in the world today is extraordinary, particularly in the type of machines and machinery used to perform all types of tasks. Farm equipment is no exception. The advancement and ingenuity that have been designed and manufactured for agricultural use today are incredible.

Take, for instance, the manner in which grain is harvested. Much has changed from the days when a sickle was used to cut the grain stalk, which was then bundled, hauled to a threshing machine, which then would separate the grain from the chaff. This was only possible with grains such as wheat, oats, barley, and others of this type. It was a laborious process with many required steps to end up with grain. The grain itself was then, of course, used for animal feed as well as a product used in producing many types of food consumed by mankind. The chaff had little use beyond that of being used as bedding for animals.

Today's modern combines cut grain stalks of all types (wheat and even corn), gathers them into a mechanism that shakes the grain free from the chaff, empties them into a large storage bin while the chaff, stalks and husks alike are distributed evenly in the field to serve as a nutrient for future crops, or otherwise bailed for such uses as bedding and fodder for animals. Through agricultural engineering and research, the grain itself, as well as the chaff, is used in beneficial ways today.

In the world in which we live, it is common to look at life from the perspective of *good* and *evil*. We associate good as being positive, rewarding, joyful, and fulfilling, while evil is generally thought of as being negative, demeaning, and useless if not harmful. That is much like the grain which has worth, while the chaff is a solid waste or fodder. Just as a combine separates the two and agricultural engineers create ways for its use, God is able to use good and evil to His advantage. It is obvious as to how God uses good in our personal lives, in the world around us, and throughout the entire universe. Although it is not so obvious as to how God uses evil in a beneficial way.

The most common way in which God can use "Evil for Good" is in the consequences, perceived or real, that generally result from it. It is those results that God uses to demonstrate the rewards of living in ways that are good. Be it an accident, health issue, or some other personal calamity, evil can generally be associated with having caused or effected the negative outcome in some way. God, as the Holy Spirit, acts like the farmer's combine. God separates the good from the evil. The good is used by God to bless and uplift man. The evil is discarded and self-destructs.

This is particularly the case when a person or group of people experience the consequences of an act of evil caused by others. God, in some way, will bring out the good to overshadow the bad. It may take a day, week, month, or even years before it is realized that there was, in fact, a positive and good side to what happened. God will never allow evil to persist and go on indefinitely. The root of the evil may cause the outgrowth to reemerge at a new time and in a different form, but God is prepared to defeat and overcome it at its very source. Ultimately, something that is good, be it an act, a situation, or anything else, can never be bad, "It Is Good". Something that is evil can have an ultimate result of having produced good. That is how God, The Holy Spirit, works. What is intended to be meant for evil, God will turn it around and use it to His advantage for good!

DON'T GET IN GOD'S WAY

God has a plan for every person's life. It's a plan He has prepared each of us to be able to fulfill. We're provided with every talent, skill, and opportunity to live our lives following the path He had intended for us to follow when He instilled the Holy Spirit within each of us at conception. While God does not force His plan for our lives upon us, His desire is that we follow through with it.

As we proceed in life, the tyrannical mind is proficient in convincing us that another way is better. We end up blocking God and His plan for our life. We insist on doing it our way. We just get in God's way. Our lives become unsettled, situations threaten our serenity, and everyday challenges become overwhelming. We set ourselves up for failure and disappointment. Life becomes a living Hell.

God's plan for the life of everyone is one of love, peace, and joy, a life of good health, healing, and wholeness. In many cases one's life is over too soon before realizing the lifelong error one has made. Yet as long as one has a beating heart, a loving beating heart, the ability to fill their lungs with life-giving oxygen, and get out of God's way, the compassionate God is ready to be proactive in their life.

God never loses sight of where we are in life, even when we get in His way. Once we let down our protective shield and stop insisting on doing it our way, God is prepared to reinstall within each of us the plan He had for us from the very beginning. It may have to be adjusted, augmented with new skill opportunities and newly acquired talents, but God can do this. It's never too late to step aside, get out of God's way, and change the direction our lives are taking.

KEEP PLOWING THROUGH

Man has many tools to plow through seemingly difficult or even impossible circumstances. Some are relatively simple, yet others are very large. There are things we take for granted, such as tools and appliances. Others are much more consequential. In the winter in areas that have heavy snow, powered snowblowers are of great assistance in removing piles of heavy show. At the other extreme, huge ice breakers plow through frozen shipping lanes of thick ice to keep passageways open for commercial and military ships. The simple process of preparing the soil for planting was once burdensome and time consuming for farmers who tilled the soil by hand with the aid of oxen and horses. Today it is done by massive farm machinery, which has changed it all with massive machines designed and manufactured by companies like John Deere.

So too. . .

God has a tool to aid man in overcoming and plowing through seemingly difficult challenges. That tool is the Holy Spirit. When we Awaken the Spirit within, the spiritual strength of a loving and compassionate God gives a person the strength to make it through whatever a person may be facing in life. No matter how small or how large and seemingly overwhelming a situation may be, with God and an awakened Spirit, one has the power and might to plow their way through. The awareness of God's presence in one's life allows God's divine wisdom to enlighten them, the strength of God to empower them, and the love of God to fill their heart. No obstacle is too thwarting or challenging. With God, all things are possible. With the awareness of the ever presence of Spirit and faith, with God, one can KEEP PLOWING THROUGH.

DECLARE, FROM NOW ON, "THERE ARE NO EXCUSES"

What occupies your time? What comes first in your life? Are you more inclined to react to the call or need of someone else, before meeting your own needs?

We can't truly be of help to others when we are not at our peak ability spiritually, mentally, and physically. Requiring the highest standards of ourselves is the example others need to emulate in their own lives, personally, emotionally, psychologically, and even occupationally.

Being of service and helping others is certainly admirable, and there are people in our lives that we should reach out to in any way we are able. Focused on the situations of others though, may be an escape from admitting and addressing one's own needs. Getting so busy meeting the needs and desires of others may cause us to neglect our taking care of ourselves. It may also just be an *EXCUSE* to direct our attention from things in our persona that we should be addressing.

It can be convenient to look at ourselves, compare the way we are to that of another, thereby leaning on the *EXCUSE,* "Well, I'm not as bad as so and so", or "I may have this or that bad habit, but I know I could use more self-control if I really put my mind to it". Sometimes, instead of helping others reach for and obtain their highest level of good, we are being an enabler, and in essence, approving of the very thing in their life that we should be taking better control of in our own lives.

One of the gifts we are all endowed with from God is the gift of self-control. With a strong will and self-discipline, we are able to refrain from doing the things that are detrimental to our health and negatively affect our everyday lives. While we may hold ourselves back from attaining our highest good, God will never hold us back. God is the great enabler. God not only provides each of us, through the "Power of the Holy Spirit Within", the will and ability to be raised to our highest good by making extraordinary efforts of self-improvement, He enables us to be a blessing to others.

So, *"Declare,* from now on, *There are no more Excuses"*!

Be the best you can be, then, be compassionate, giving, and a true blessing to others.

COMPLAINING

So, God,

What Am I Complaining About?

I Released Myself to You,

I Asked You to Use Me,

You Did,

and Now I'm Complaining,

Go Figure!

REMOTE STARTER

A handy device in vehicles, particularly in areas with extreme temperatures, is a feature that remotely and automatically starts the vehicle's engine. From inside a house, building, or wherever, a person can activate the device that will turn on the engine of their vehicle, activating the appropriate climate control settings, allowing the interior of the vehicle to warm up or cool down. Thereby, the person will have a nice comfortable vehicle to get into when they're ready to leave for their destination.

Sometimes, we need to use a "Remote Starter" with God. Like the vehicle sitting there waiting to be started, God is there as the Holy Spirit waiting to be activated in a person's life. A person has to take action by opening their heart and mind to the will of God through prayer and meditation. These are the "Remote Starters" that will activate God, who is ever ready to take you to the destination He has for your life.

RACE TRACK

As a novice attending a high-speed driver training school, learning to drive a powerful and fast sports car on a closed road track, the experience can be exhilarating. Typically, the school starts with several hours of classroom instruction. Then you have a real-time experience, in a car designed for racing, with an experienced race driver as your instructor in the passenger seat. The instructor coaches you as you progressively gain confidence in yourself and begin to appreciate what the car can do. With a few laps around the track, and a few like sessions on the track, as your skill level becomes more proficient, at some point the instructor sets you free to solo for a few laps, all the time under the instructor's watchful eye from an observation point.

Over a three-day school one gets the thrill of what it's like to reach high speeds, break hard to enter into the curves, and apply rapid acceleration to speed down a straightaway. Then, to repeat the process again and again over the length of the track.

Then comes the real treat. Midday on the last day of the school, you're invited to ride with your instructor in the instructor's personal race car and make several laps around the track, as a passenger. Well, you want exhilaration? You quickly realize that no matter how proficient you may have thought you have become, and no matter how confident you may have become in your own abilities, the real thrill is relinquishing the controls to the expert.

Strange as it may seem, there is an interesting parallel in our lives and in the way we relate to God. Sure, in life, particularly if we are in faith and trust God's guiding hand, we may live a wonderful and fulfilling life and please God in many ways in the things we do. But then, there is always that thing about being in control, being in the driver's seat, taking, or at least making, a good attempt of directing our life.

However, when we release ourselves to God and turn the driver's seat over to God, we will be on the ride of our life. God will take us to places we would have never even imagined we might go. Yes, we may live our lives experiencing many thrills and satisfying experiences on our own. Yet, when we release ourselves to God, the heights we'll experience will far exceed anything we may have experienced on our own.

However, like the race instructor who is there to coach us in the skills of high-speed racing, God is there to coach, train, and prepare us for the race of life. As with the race instructor, when we are fully prepared, God releases us to pursue the path He has directed us to follow. As we pursue that path, we are always under the watchful eye of God, our Instructor, who is at the ready to step in to provide guiding instructions and to keep us from deviating from the clear direction He has for our lives. Even if we persist in following the direction the tyrannical mind leads and disaster is the ultimate consequence, God is always there to pick up the pieces and guide us through healing and restoration, putting our life back together and on the direct path He has for our lives.

FOR ME OR WITH ME

I'd Much Rather Know that God Is with Me

Because

If God Is with Me,

I'm Sure He's for Me!

TAKE LIFE IN STRIDE

The daily and even weekly routine in many of our lives sometimes becomes a repetitive schedule we just automatically allow ourselves to become accustomed to. Starting our day at approximately the same time, having the same foods for breakfast, taking the same route to work or wherever, fulfilling the same tasks and so on.

Then suddenly, without warning, an unexpected event or situation will cause us to have to change one or more of those routines. We will experience anxious moments, periods of uncertainty, doubt, fear, hesitation, and even times when we come to a complete halt. What we once took for granted as the way things were, they no longer are.

There are times that major events do affect our lives. A serious accident or medical occurrence in our life or in the life of a relative or close friend may require us to completely alter our schedule for a time. A change in a relationship or job may cause us to radically change our coarse in life. An unexpected financial situation may cause us to alter our lifestyle for a period.

Many things we encounter in life however, aren't that consequential. Yet we are inclined sometimes to allow these less significant events to take a much more distracting role and break our stride. We can be distracted by undue worry and concern, mulling over a situation, or an anticipated situation, over and over. We can become overly concerned about what can and may happen and how we will handle it.

Living every moment of our lives "Awakened to the Power of the Holy Spirit Within" enables us to maintain our stride. We are able to continue unaffected by these feelings and concerns. We only need to be concerned in doing "What It Is That It Is Ours to do", then leave the rest up to God.

"Let your eyes look directly forward, and your gaze be straight before you". Proverbs 4:25 (ESV)

CALLING AN ASSOCIATE!

One day I went into a Big Box DIY store to purchase a certain product in the paint department. The five-gallon item I needed to buy was out of stock on the shelf where it was normally available. Knowing from experience that there may be more on the top of the shelving display, where overstock was often stored, I saw more of the item.

Seeking the assistance of a store associate, we returned to the area of the item, and the associate agreed to get a high lift to bring the overstocked item down in order that I might purchase it. In a very short time he returned with an elevator type electrically operated high lift. He positioned it, boarded the lift, attached all the safety devices, raised himself to the upper shelf, and loaded two cans of the item onto the platform of the lift.

A short time passed, and then he told me that he couldn't get the lift to operate and lower itself back to floor level. He intimated that because it was April Fool's Day, I must be jinxed. Perhaps I wasn't meant to purchase the item, and he was going to end up being stuck up there. Just at that time, a second associate walked by. Without hesitation and without other words being exchanged, he said to the first associate, "Turn it off and back on, it's been giving us trouble, they have to fix that thing", and continued on his way. Sure enough, the associate helping me turned the switch off and back on, pushed the down button, and the equipment functioned perfectly lowering the associate and my product to the floor level.

Reflecting on the situation later, it dawned on me that this was no chance occurrence. When we live aware of the "Awakened Power of the Holy Spirit Within", God is not only active in our lives, but also in the lives of others with whom we associate.

The second associate didn't just happen to be passing by at that particular time by chance. His recognizing the circumstances and having the knowledge of what was happening and what to do about it, wasn't simply coincidence. He could have been any place else in the store at that time. The first associate may not have had knowledge of the equipment having failed to operate properly in the past, and even then, may not have known how to resolve the problem.

This is simply another example of being blessed by God, not only to bring the right people at the right time across our paths, but also bless those with whom we interact, bringing the right people across their path at exactly the right time for the right purpose. I can visualize God "Calling an Associate"! God knew the knowledgeable associate to call the minute the need presented itself.

How ironic that this happened April First. I have always believed and experienced the fact that God has a great sense of humor. Perhaps the experience was a brief exposure of that humor when at first I was led to believe that the store was out of product and I had wasted a trip going there. Then when the lift failed, while only a minute passed until it became operable again, God laughingly was saying, "Got-cha-again"! It always bothers me when God gets the best of me and I visualize God waltzing around Heaven given the angels and saints high fives! Yes, even God can play April Fool's Jokes.

SQUARE PEG IN A ROUND HOLE

Give a young child a square peg and a board with several different sized and shaped holes in it, and it's amazing how the child will generally be entertained and persistent in attempting to find a hole the square peg will go into. Yes, some may get frustrated and give up or at least find a large enough round hole in which to put their peg. Remove all the square holes except the one the child's peg will fit in, leaving all the round holes, and it is amazing how quickly the child will recognize the significance of the shape of the holes and place the peg in the appropriate square hole.

Also amazing is how as adults we often fail to learn this simple lesson. Square pegs do not fit in round holes, and if they do, they probably aren't where they belong. We can look at ourselves as square pegs, (no insult intended) and look at our options in life as holes we may insert ourselves into. Whether pursuing an education, an occupation, or any life choice, such as remaining single or having a partner, raising a family, even recreational, dietary, and spare time activities, some are a perfect fit, others we aren't able to fit into at all, and in some we just seem to rattle around.

Sometimes an area we think is the right fit, or we want to be the right fit, just doesn't work out. Other times a choice comes too easy and proves unsatisfying once we get immersed in it. Usually it does take a little trial and error before finding the proper fit. When we find the right hole in which to insert our peg, so to speak, everything just feels right. That doesn't mean that everything is always prefect and without friction or challenges. With a little elbow grease the peg slips right into its hole. That "elbow grease" may include a learning process, assistance from others, and very likely, the hand of God providing the supernatural gifts that make things all come together in accordance with His plan for your life.

God gave each person the gifts in the form of talents and skills to achieve and fulfill the plan He has for our life. Nothing has been left out or forgotten by God with which you will need to put the square peg in the right hole. A person can become disenchanted, give up, or accept a situation that they can fit into, yet never feel satisfied that it is the proper fit. Many times, accepting the status quo, yet feeling that there is still something out there that is a better fit, simply leads a person to be lackadaisical. Yes, we get by, but never feel that satisfaction that gives us that good feeling about ourselves. God's desire is for every person to be fulfilled and use His gifts in the way in which each of us, with peace and joy, awaken each new day with anticipation and enthusiasm.

God never abandons a person who seeks His guidance and strives to do what it is that they are called to do in order to fulfill His plan for their life. Through the "Awakened Power of the Holy Spirit Within", trying to put the "Square Peg in the Round Role" won't be the never-ending quest resulting in continual rejection or failed attempts. You will be guided to be at the right place at the right time for the right reason. Your peg will find the perfect hole.

A SIMPLE LITTLE DROP OF WATER

On a beautiful October day, while driving along the Blue Ridge Parkway in North Carolina checking out the fall colors, we came upon an overlook at about 3,200 feet elevation which provided a beautiful view of the valley below and the mountains in the distance covered in beautiful fall colors.

However, it was the site on the opposite side of the road that caught my attention. Rising up from road level for perhaps a hundred feet or more was a solid rock formation standing majestically. A park Ranger pointed out and described a carnivorous animal-eating plant clinging to the rock, and sure enough a small bug was snared by the plant and the bug disappeared.

That was amazing and interesting to witness. However, the things that really attracted my attention were the small drops of water seemingly coming out of solid rock. As they dripped and flowed down the rock to the ground, a very small stream was created, which flowed off in a distance and out of sight.

Somewhat overcome by the wonder of these small drops of water, I could only ponder that this was an example of the mighty hand and goodness of God in action as the small drops of water were;

> . . .leading to a stream, creating a lake, poring over a majestic waterfall into a flowing river and winding its way to an ocean. . .
> in the process of interacting with the sun and wind, producing clouds and rain, resulting in lush landscapes, healthy life-forms, plentiful food supplies, nourishment, and the survival of life itself.

PRAISE GOD FOR EVERY LITTLE SIMPLE DROP OF WATER

BUILT FROM SCRATCH

Hobbyists and people who are creative often build things from scratch. This is a term used to indicate that they are using their creative abilities. A person starts with basic materials and supplies and creates the item they have imagined and pictured in their mind. A lady who works with cloth and thread may sew a dress, shirt, or some other type of clothing. One who works with thread may knit a scarf, a doily, or some other colorful and intricate piece of handiwork. A person interested in model trains may use small pieces of wood, plastic, or metal and build a small-scale model train car, building, or even an entire scene of a town with a railroad running through it. A parent may build a miniature house with all the furniture and appropriate fixtures and thrill a young person with it as a gift, providing hours of imaginative and playful enjoyment.

The common characteristic of each of these people is their ability to combine items in a craft-full way to build or make something. They possess the knowledge of every piece and part, every way in which to use them, and every method necessary to combine them and or put them together in order to complete their project. Interesting thing is, if the item, once completed and in use as it was intended to be used, is damaged or in some way broken or disfigured, the creator of the item knows exactly what it took to create it, construct it, and consequently knows everything that is necessary to repair, fix, and return it to its original condition. In some cases, they make it better than it may have even been in the first place,

Well, well, well, guess what!! The Creator of our bodies was somewhat of an awesome scratch builder Himself! Take one's body or any part of it, having been created by God, isn't it He who knows every minute part, how its put together, its purpose and how its intended to work? So therefore, if any part of the body should break down and need repair, isn't God the expert who knows exactly what it is that needs to be done to fix it? Our amazing God not only knows what has to be done, but exactly what it takes to make the repairs and perhaps even make it better.

God has not only blessed man with the ability to develop medicines, instruments, and procedures, but also the people with the skills to administer and perform incredible repairs of the human body. It is the mind of man, however, that is the most amazing gift man has been given by God. Why? Because all the medicines, skills, and procedures in the world may repair or even replace body parts, but it is the mind that enables healing. It is the indwelling Spirit of God in unison with the mind that provides the ability to overcome adversities, be they physical, emotional, or psychological, and cure even the most threatening human challenges a person may face.

Yes, as the Master "Scratch Builder," God knows every intricate part of every single person, what each part consists of, how it's put together, and how He intended for it to work. God surely is the one who knows what it takes to mend, repair, or replace broken parts. A person may require the help of medicines, procedures, and skilled technicians to carry out the necessary steps in a given situation. It is God however, who through the Holy Spirit within enables the mind to provide the power of healing.

Thank You, God!

THE GREAT BLUE HERON
(The giraffe of the bird world)

With long lanky legs, a slender body, a long neck extended upward like that of a giraffe, and a small protruding head, **The Great Blue Heron** struts along the shoreline near the water searching for its prey. However in flight, The Great Blue Heron folds its legs in, bends its neck in a U shape, and brings its head back close to the body, creating a sleek, compact bird in flight with a large wingspan that enables it to fly with a slow regular beat of its wings. It isn't at all obvious when it is on the ground strutting around what a large wingspan it has.

Remind you of anyone? At times, we come in contact with people who may remind us of the Great Blue Heron. They are just "So Perfect"! At least that's the perception they want others to have of them and acknowledge. It's that "Look at Me" air they carry about themselves. Most are very likely genuinely nice people, and perhaps the opinion that others may have of them is unfairly judgmental. There could also be a certain amount of jealously. You think?

Perhaps, if we took the time to get to know them personally, their "real self" is not like that at all. They may be more like the graceful Great Blue Heron in flight, confident but not arrogant, compassionate and understanding with a big heart, tending to their own business without meddling into the affairs of others. Is what we're perceiving a product of our own bias and judgment? Are we looking at another and actually making a comparison with which we will attempt to raise the level of our own self-worth above that of others?

It is we ourselves, sometimes, who need to reflect upon how we present ourselves to others. God made each person unique in their own special way. God wants us to be appreciative and accepting of that uniqueness in others. That doesn't mean that we must agree with them, or that we have to have a desire to associate with someone we feel uncomfortable around. They may not have any interest in associating with us either, and that's okay.

Yet sometimes, it may be that very person who for a specific reason, God is allowing to pass through our path in life. If we took the opportunity to get to know the person, we may find that they are able to make a real contribution to and in our lives. On the other hand, perhaps God is alerting us to take a good look at ourselves and consider some important changes we need to make in our life.

Nothing in life happens by chance, really! Either we have made a direct, sometimes indirect, purposeful choice or non-choice. Or God, for a purpose we may not understand, has brought forth a situation to achieve His objectives in and for our lives. God gave the Great Blue Heron the ability to walk in a purposeful way while surveying the entire area around it while on the ground, and yet, in the air, fly gracefully with seemingly little effort. God also made each one of us to be purposeful and graceful, each in our own way.

NEED STUFF

Even God needs "Stuff" to work with if you expect Him to be proactive in your life.

We need "STUFF" to build things, a lot of "STUFF." To bake bread (flour), make pottery (clay), a car (steel), a house (wood), towns (people), cities (buildings), and in every case a lot more than the single most important ingredient.

So if we want God to be active in our lives, we have to provide Him the "STUFF" that He has already provided us to work with. The basic ingredient is the "Spirit Within". By "Awakening the Power of the Holy Spirit Within", we release the talents and skills God has gifted us with.

Each of us is unique and has specific gifts that God can use to accomplish supernatural things in our lives, and through us in the lives of others. They may be things considered by some as ordinary and routine. Bread is thought of as being ordinary, yet we use it in a reference as "The Bread of Life", when talking about life and important aspects of life. God uses the "ordinary" things in our lives in extraordinary ways.

Each talent and skill we have has been given to us in order to fulfill the plan God has for our life. Whether His plan is for us to live a quiet life, going about our daily responsibilities dutifully and competently, or our life stands out among our piers. Whether we are a loving parent to our children or a community leader responsible for the welfare of the lives of many. God gives each of us the "wherewithal" to "get-it-done".

No matter what our role in life, it is not only important to use those God given talents, but it is equally important to hone them and use them to their greatest extent. "STUFF" made into things will decay, deteriorate, become broken or lost if not used and maintained properly.

In the same way a plant will wither and die if left without water and sunlight, our skills and talents, not used, nurtured, and honed through their application in fulfilling God's plan for our life, will fade and become useless to us.

Open your life to God in order that He might use your "STUFF," and "get-it-done."

OVER TIME

Living with an awakened Spirit within may not appear to have an impact or be obvious in one's life. Over time, however, the manner in which one faces and handles everyday occurrences and challenges will make it obvious that the Spirit within, God, is taking an active role in one's life.

Situations in the past, which otherwise would have caused nervousness, anger, frustration, and even caused a person to strike out to hurt others or be revengeful, now are taken in stride. Instead of being judgmental of how another is interacting with you, compassion and understanding soothe reactions and eases tension.

God is our mediator, the one who understands every facet of our situation and that of another. God knows how to achieve consensus and mutual understanding and create in every situation a result that will favor everyone involved.

Continually living one's life seeking to raise the "Awareness of the Power of the Holy Spirit of God Within" eventually will become an influence in every phase and activity in one's life. At the time when life and the activities of life unfold, it may not be obvious the role and significance "The Power of the Holy Spirit Within" takes. However, when one looks back at a later time, be it a few moments, hours, days, months, and sometimes even years, one will be amazed and realize God never failed to be there taking an active role in all that happened.

SPECIAL ASSISTANCE NEEDED

"Special Assistance Needed!
Special Assistance Needed
in Isle 23"!

Sometimes heard over the Public Address System in a Big Box Store.

That is what God does in our lives when we sometimes need to go beyond the ordinary.

Through the Supernatural Gifts God is able to provide for us at difficult or challenging times, He provides the Special Assistance we need to see our way through.

PRAYER INTERCESSOR[1]

Have you ever had the name or a vision of a person come to mind for no apparent reason? Perhaps a family member or friend, a coworker, or acquaintance from long ago, or even some personality or sports figure.

At first you may just ignore the thought. Then though, you may think about the person and the circumstances in which they played in your life, or yours in theirs. Then, allowing the thought to pass and the memory to fade, you go on with what you were doing, dismissing the whole situation.

Generally, we may be quick to respond to a situation in our lives or in the life of someone close to us by turning to God in prayer, even at unusual or inconvenient times. A little prayer asking for guidance, wholeness, relief, or peace. However, God also calls upon us to ask His guidance and blessings upon others, perhaps people we don't even know.

When the thought of that person comes to mind, stopping, if only for a moment, to beseech God's goodness in their lives or the situation they or someone significant to them is a part of, is answering God's call that they are in need of prayer. It may mean hundreds, thousands, or even millions of people from all around the world may have been called, and answered His plea, and prayed for that individual and their situation.

What is even more astounding is to consider that if so many are praying to God for the needs of that person, in your time of need, God will request and have millions of people from all around the world, in many languages, yet in one Spirit, who don't even know you, praying for you.

Answer God's call, whenever and for whoever it may be, and be a Prayer Intercessor!

[1] Prayer Intercessor: The act of praying to God on behalf of others.

The Apostle Paul's exhortation to Timothy specified that intercession prayers can be made for those in authority.

"I urge, then, first of all, that petitions, prayers, intercession and thanksgiving be made for all people—for Kings and all those in authority, that we may live peaceful and quiet lives in all godliness and holiness."

1 Timothy 2:1–2 (NIV)

THE SHOOTING GALLERY

Festivals, fairs, and amusements parks often have an attraction such as a Shooting Gallery. Some have a variety of figures, such as animals running across and appearing randomly in a backdrop. A person can use a special rifle to shoot at the animals, and if accurately aimed and shot at, an animal will be knocked down, or may respond in some other way, and the person will be rewarded with a prize. The prize may be a stuffed animal or some appropriate trinket suitable for the degree of difficulty the shooter has demonstrated.

The jubilant participant walks away proudly displaying their reward so others are able to witness their prowess in having conquered the challenge of the Shooting Gallery. The prize, if it even makes it to the home of the participant, is placed and proudly displayed in a prominent place on a shelf or perhaps in a chair. Remaining there, it will be a reminder of the accomplishment and be a showcase of the achievement to others. In time however, it is overlooked, becomes dusty or tattered, and eventually is forgotten and even discarded.

The little animals at the Shooting Gallery however, just keep popping up, allowing others to keep taking potshots at them. The attraction may have moved on to another festival or fair in another town or location, but the resilient little animals continue to do their thing. They allow people to take aim at them, keep getting shot down, then walk away feeling smug and rewarded for having hit the target and knocked the animal down.

How do you feel? Like the little animal with people always taking potshots at you? Or, are you one of those people who are always trying to put others down, attempting to win the prize at the expense of others you knock down. The real winners are the ones who get knocked down and spring right back up.

They are the ones who move on, find another place to set up, and go about doing their thing. They realize and accept that there will always be people who will be shooting at them to feel better about themselves and showing off their prize.

The short-term feelings of satisfaction one experiences by attempting to build themselves up while tearing another down only contributes to their own downward spiral. A place where they will eventually find themselves at a point or below, where they had attempted to lower another. We have been placed on this earth as brothers and sisters to help one another, to pick another up when they are down, and encourage them when they are in need.

God, who is loving and compassionate, blesses those who are supportive of others and watches over those who are suppressed and put down.

"Blessed are those who are persecuted because of righteousness, for theirs is the kingdom of heaven". *Matthew 5:10 (NIV)*

APPRECIATE
AND
LIVE THE PRESENT

WHICH IS
PERFECTLY BALANCED BETWEEN

THE BLESSINGS OF THE PAST
and
THE PROMISES OF THE FUTURE

QUAKE AND RUMBLE

The Little Quake that Rumbles and Springs forth. It may just be a little seed or bulb in the ground. Yet, when God touches it with His mighty hand, it erupts like a volcano overflowing with undeterred might.

As flowers they are created in every design and shape imaginable and painted by God in an endless rainbow of colors. As trees they grow to majestic forms, shapes, and sizes as they reach to the heavens to praise their Creator and become a source of food, shelter, and endless resources to be appreciated and made use of by the creativity of man.

And Man? When touched by the loving hand of God through the Holy Spirit, man erupts as an instrument of God's love and peace, overflowing like the volcano with actions of kindness, fellowship, support, help, and guidance.

THE LADDER

There are many types of ladders that can be used in a large number of situations. Their general purpose is to raise a person to a higher position to achieve a given purpose or task. Most have caution and/or warning signs that advise a person that climbing all the way to the very top, the upper rungs or levels of the ladder, can potentially be dangerous, because one may lose their balance and fall, causing great harm or even death.

Properly using the ladder to elevate oneself to a comfortable position, one can complete the desired task they have set out to perform. Then, gradually, one step at a time, descend safely and without incident to the point at which they had begun. That is not to say that a person may ascend to the very top of a ladder, achieve their objective, then remain there for a period of time, before descending to the point they were at originally.

Regardless, once one has reached the top of the ladder there are only two options—remain where they are or go back down. They may have reason, or the desire, to reach greater heights than the ladder they are using will allow. However, without returning to the bottom and securing a new ladder, or some sort of extension for the current ladder, they will be stuck where they are at the top.

Life can be like that as well. Climbing the ladder of success, economically, socially, or even spiritually, one can reach levels impossible to go beyond without stepping back and starting over, sometimes from the very bottom. One may find themselves in a situation such as being on the top rung of the ladder and having no place to go but back down. For some, a situation like this may be devastating and difficult to accept or even recover from. For others it may turn out to be a blessing in disguise, providing the opportunity to rise to even greater heights.

It takes a positive attitude and faith in God to enable a person to set aside the things of the past, close that page of their life, take advantage of the experience, and start over. God's plan for each of our lives is to be victors and achievers. We glorify God by putting our trust in His plan for our life and for the way in which He has set out to use the talents and skills He has blessed each of us with. Whether at the top of ladder, on the way up or even at the bottom looking up, trust in the Holy Spirit of God to show the way. He may raise you to a higher level than you ever believed possible.

GOD'S VERSATILITY

God is able to Push us, Pull us, Carry us, and Walk beside us.

When we are reluctant to keep moving forward in the direction God has for our lives, we may tend to want to hold back and be hesitant to move forward. We may be frightened by what we can't see which lies over the hill in the road ahead. There may be frightening things that we imagine are threatening along the way. In which case, God gets behind us and pushes us on along the path we're following.

Then there are the times we just positively refuse to follow that path God has for us. We insist on following a path of our own. We go on a path that we think is more rewarding and more pleasurable, and we struggle. We may be persuaded by others to follow them, forget the way God has laid out for us, and seek worldly rewards, and we struggle. Yet, God is able to tie His concern around us, pull us along the path He has laid out for us, and keep us moving in the right direction.

O' my, at times we may just refuse to even move in any direction. We conclude we are happy, content, and totally secure right where we are. We look around and see a lot of unknowns out there, and put on blinders, refusing to even consider that God may have a better place with incredible blessings awaiting us, if we simply move on from where we are. So, God simply wraps His loving arms around us, picks us up, and carries us along the path to the place He has laid out for us and our future.

Most amazing of all, though, is when God walks side by side with us down that path of life. Hand and hand with God the road ahead spans off into the distance. Though there may be hills and valleys, they are of modest consequence and present no particular difficulty. Along the path we see beautiful flowers laid out like a border of carpet keeping us on the path that sparkles with diamond-like jewels beneath each footstep we take. Off in the distance to either side, we catch the glimpse of animals scampering off gleefully as the serenade of birds fill the air with a joyful sound of greetings. Along the pathway we see familiar faces of smiling people we cherish as loving family, supportive friends, friendly strangers, greeting us and expressing assuredness that the path we're on and the companion by our side are truly a wondrous thing to behold.

As far as that friend is concerned, well, the love, support, guidance, and the fact that He is committed to being there under all circumstances is not only reassuring but incredible. He shares His thoughts in our thoughts, His emotions through His compassion with our emotions. His joy with our joy and sorrow with His understanding. Considering that at times we have been stubborn, bullheaded, and just down right uncooperative, He has always still been there, and always will be, *to Push us, Pull us, and Carry us.*

Thank You, Lord !

THE LASER

Some newer circular saws and other power equipment now come with a fancy new laser beam that shows you the path to follow to get the perfect result. You still have to guide the saw or the piece being cut, but at least you can directly see the path the saw will take if you follow the line put down by the laser. Previously, a person had to focus on the blade itself or markings on the saw to follow a previously drawn line in the piece being cut to get the desired results. With the laser projected out front of the saw, one is led in the direction the saw will take and therefore less likely to stray from the direct path, achieving a more consistent cut one desires to attain. In some particular models, you do have to move the switch to turn on the little laser light.

The same thing takes place when one has the "Awakened Power of the Holy Spirit Within". Trusting in the guidance of God, a path to follow is projected out before a person directing the way to go in order to live out the plan that God has for a person's life. Before we are even born, God has instilled within each of us that plan and the role He has for us to fulfill in our lives. God also provides us with every conceivable gift we need in order to fulfill that plan. The primary gift is the Holy Spirit Within, which is ever present to be switched on like the laser light, to direct the path we take in life.

Like the laser light that is there to help guide us, the Holy Spirit is also always there to be switched on to help guide us. However, we sometimes ignore or forget we have the availability and the guidance of the Holy Spirit. Just as we may forget to activate the laser light, we may not remember to activate the Holy Spirit, through prayer and meditation, in order to take advantage of following the clear direction God has for our lives. When we do forget, the tyrannical mind can, and often does, lead us off coarse and we end up messing up our lives.

We find that we have to back up and start over again using and following a whole new plan. Just like when we fail to use the laser light to guide our saw and mess up a nice piece of wood, then have to discard it and start all over again with a new piece of wood.

God didn't place us on this earth without providing us with everything we need, including a line to be followed, in order to fulfill His plan for our lives. A plan of peace, joy, and fulfillment. Switch on the laser, "Awaken the Power of the Holy Spirit Within" and be guided to your highest good.

FAITH – PHOTO CELL

Electrical current

A relationship with God is somewhat like electrical current. The flow of electricity to, through, and returning from an electrical fixture or light bulb, to the source from which it came is what makes the fixture operate or the bulb glow.

So it is with our relationship with God. The grace of God flows to us continuously. It is up to us to flip the switch to let the grace and love of God flow through us and return to Him, the source, through our appreciation, thankfulness, and praise.

God's grace illuminates and inspires us to light up our lives and the world around us. Thereby we fulfill His plan of action and activities in our lives in a way that is pleasing to Him and follows the direction He has for our lives.

Photocell

There are times however in life that circumstances keep us from being all God had intended for us to be. We may become discouraged, let down, feel defeated, or lack inspiration, ambition, or motivation to fulfill a task or actively move in a positive direction.

It is in times like this that we fail to flip that switch that will allow the flow of God's grace to flow through us and rejuvenate and keep us moving in the direction He has for our lives. Things become bleak and a darkness overcomes us.

When this begins to happen, like the photocell that automatically turns on the light to activate the flow of electricity and illuminate the area, our faith in God, His love for us, and our faith in ourselves activate the flow of God's grace in our lives.

Light Up a Darkened Area

Not all lights have photocells to switch on and allow the flow of electricity to illuminate it. However, a photocell can be connected to any light so that it will operate automatically to light up an area when darkness sets in.

Likewise, not everyone has faith. A person can make that connection through prayer and the awareness of God's love for them. Awakening faith in our lives through the power of the Holy Spirit, in order that the Grace of God will automatically flow through us at a time we feel disconnected, will illuminate our lives and move us in a positive direction according to God's plan for our lives.

A HUG FROM GOD

Do you need a hug from God? Wouldn't you just love it if you could get a real hands-on honest to goodness hug from God. When you're feeling down, discouraged, disappointed, defeated, wouldn't it be nice to get a hug from God. Even when something extraordinary happens unexpectedly, or a long tedious project comes to a successful conclusion, wouldn't you just love it if you could get a real hands-on honest to goodness hug from God.

When Jesus Christ walked among the people, His loving hug to those He embraced was a hug from God. Have you stopped to consider, God didn't stop giving hugs once Christ was gone. God continues to freely embrace us through the hugs of the people in our lives. Whether it's a greeting or at a time of departure, that warm hug is a hug from God. When someone hugs us in a time of sorrow or misfortune, accomplishment, or victory, that's a hug from God.

We may sometimes, and possibly in all situations, shy away from those hugs and perhaps not feel free to return the gesture. Could it be said that we are turning our back on God and His desire to show His love for us? How unfortunate that would be. On the other hand, are we ourselves refusing to be God's loving arms by not hugging another? Just as God showered His love upon people through Christ, God's desire is to use every one of us to spread His love among us.

God knows our needs. God's desire is to meet those needs. God's only resource to satisfy His desire to fulfill those needs is through the members of His Holy body. Not only when we or others are experiencing bad times, but in good times as well. God isn't interested in being standoffish, God wants to be right in the middle of things. While it is believed that God can do anything and everything, He can't physically touch and hug us except through our willingness to hug and be supportive of one another. Are you allowing God to use you? Hug someone today. Hay, why not hug a whole bunch today!

CRACK IN THE WALL

In life we at times
face barriers or obstacles
we just can't find a way
to get around, over, or through.
They can be those
we set up ourselves by our actions
or even by our lack of action.
Our all-knowing loving God knows where
the "Cracks in the wall" are
and has the way and the perfect plan to
Push us Through

WHEN THINGS STAND STILL

During the planting, growing, and harvesting seasons, a farmer is a busy person. When the final harvest has been completed, those unfamiliar with the agriculture industry and the real lives of a farmer may assume that the farmer has a few months to relax. Some expect that they may even take a long, deserved luxury vacation away from the farm.

Fortunately for us who depend on the crops produced by the people in agriculture, that just isn't the case. They may take a short well-deserved hiatus from the ranch, so to speak; however, soon it is back to work. First the farmer analyzes the results of the harvest as compared to earlier years. Then comes the job of following market prices to determine the best time to take product to market to make a fair profit. Then the preparation for a new season, which comes only too soon. There is time spent in repairing, cleaning, changing fluids in equipment, then procuring the product for planting and the nutrients to be added to the soil to produce the best result. Needless to say, the farmer doesn't sit around in the off season doing nothing.

Our lives can be compared with the farmers. When things are moving rapidly and full of activity, we become all wrapped up in the events of planning, preparing, and following through in order to be certain that everything produces the result for which we strive.

Then as things do come to fruition and everything seems to slow down to a normal routine, we may ask, "What's next"? We know that God is always working behind the scenes in our lives creating opportunities and challenges. We will likely be busily involved with some new task or project soon enough. But in the meantime, what now?

Perhaps, like the farmer, that is a time for us to prepare ourselves for what God has in our future. We may pay special attention to our spiritual life, our health, our general welfare. It may be an opportunity to spend time communicating with God through meditation or by reading inspirational writings or books. *(i.e. **"Releasing your life willingly and Purposefully to God" by L. Patrick Kastner**).*

Having a busy life, we may have neglected our health. Becoming involved in a health club or in regular exercise program will strengthen our bodies for challenges that lie ahead. There may be areas in our finances, the upkeep of certain belongings, or other material possessions we have neglected to stay on top of and need our attention.

Surely, a time of repose is a gift from God, a time of preparation for what lies ahead. Yes, WHEN THINGS STAND STILL, we can relax, just go with the flow, and be comfortable in our routine. But will we be prepared to do our best when the planting season arrives? When God calls us to plant, nourish, and harvest, will we be worthy of the blessings God has prepared for us? Like a farmer makes a fair profit for the excellent crops he takes to market, our profit from God is in the many blessings He serendipitously bestows upon us.

SHADOW OF DARKNESS

It is generally accepted that where there is light, one is likely to find shadows. However, have you ever stood in a light so bright and engulfing that there was absolutely no shadow.

That is what happens when one awakens the Spirit of God within. When the Holy Spirit is shining down upon you and filling your life with His grace, there will be no shadow or darkness in your life or to be cast out from you.

However, as you move away from that light shadows begin to form. The farther one wonders and moves away from the light, the more pronounced those shadows become.

When one allows themselves to be separated from the Holy Spirit, it begins to block out the light and allows shadows of darkness to become cast out from them. Entering into the complete darkness of evil, there is no light, no shadow.

Move away from the darkness, "Awaken to the Power of the Spirit Within", and you will have the restored strength through the Grace of God to fend off evil and light up your life.

So long as the good Lord gives me the ability to put one foot in front of the other, I will be okay, as long as He guides the direction of **each step I take!**

HIGH DIVER

It is an incredible sight to watch an Olympic High Diver leave a stationary platform 33 feet (10 m) from the water, perform acrobatic stunts, and enter the water with such grace. It's obvious that they have spent years preparing for these events and developing their skills.

An athlete likely began at a very young age, and with that first jump from the side of the pool, became motivated to want to do it again and again. Next from the diving board a few feet above the water. Then after coaching, encouragement, gaining self-confidence, and skill, the jumps became higher and higher with added acrobatic feats being included.

From Olympic platforms 20 feet (6 m) long by 6.6 ft (2 m) wide, a distance from the water of 1 m (3.3 ft), 3 m (9.8 ft) and 10 m (33 ft) divers perform their skills of skewing their bodies in a free fall performing acrobatic stunts of somersaults and twists. Being judged by every aspect of the dive, a competitor must achieve perfection to be a winner.

It is not unlikely that as a diver stands on that platform preparing for a dive, a split second of doubt may enter their mind. It is quickly overshadowed however, by the visualization of every move they anticipate making as they leave the platform. Then comes the release and the intuitive reactions necessary for achieving the perfect dive, trusting in their practice, training, and total development as an athlete.

Our faith in God is much like that of the diver. We don't start off in life taking big jumps in trust and faith that God has control and is doing everything to guide us on the perfect path in life. As time passes, though, we begin to realize how God has helped us in small ways as we exercise little jumps of faith. As we take bigger and more aggressive steps in the role God plays in our lives. Our confidence grows in the expectation that God is there, we're not alone, and with His support and guidance, we can do this.

Even when we commit ourselves to God's faithful hand by releasing ourselves to His plan for our lives, there are times of hesitation and doubt. With the "Awakened Power of the Holy Spirit Within". we have the confidence to visualize right outcomes. We instinctively accept that God's plan for our lives, and every experience we are faced with encountering, is in His hands. We have come to have faith in knowing that God's plan is for our good and not for evil.

Even though our tyrannical mind may try to create doubt, may attempt to say there is another way, perhaps a better way, we're prepared for the high jump. We know God has prepared us for every opportunity and challenge in life and stands with us to see us through. Once a diver leaves that platform, nothing stands between them and the water, except their own doubts, that could prevent them from performing the perfect dive. Once we embark on an event in life, nothing stands between us and fulfillment, except our own doubts, which could prevent us from fulfilling God's plan.

As a diver reflects on the successful performances of the past, they assure themselves that this next dive will be as good as, if not, the best performance of their career. So too with God, as we reflect on the many times God has blessed us and seen us through routine and challenging times, we are able to assure ourselves that this will be no different. In the end, God's mighty hand will lead us to realizing greater accomplishments than we ever held the highest expectations of.

Even when there appears to be no
reason for hope,
keep hoping and choose to have
an Attitude of Faith and Expectancy

THE ROSEBUSH

An old scrawny rosebush, left uncared for, overgrown by weeds and shrub-bery, will produce small unappealing flowers, if any at all. If moved where it is cared for and touched by the hand of God with sunlight, nourishment, and moisture, it will eventually be restored and begin producing lush beau-tiful colorful flowers.

It is an example of a loving, restoring God, who if He will restore a simple rosebush, will certainly restore to wholeness the soul, heart, mind, and body of one of His broken, neglected, and abused children. The rosebush had to be moved from the negative surroundings that were chocking the life out of it for restoration to begin. In a like manner, we sometimes have to remove ourselves from the environment, and possibly the people, who are choking the life out of us.

Before the restoration of God can take effect, we may need to make a major change in our life and the circumstances we allow ourselves to be exposed to. Then, with the blessing of a gracious God, a forgotten individual —iso-lated, left out, and rejected by others — is able to become a blessing as the individual blooms with the love of God.

CART & BUMP
The Apple Cart
and the
Bump in the Road

In life we oftentimes find ourselves in a position where everything is looking good. Our cart is full of apples that all look bright, shinny, fresh, and very appealing. Occasionally, we may get the whiff of the smell of spoiling apples when the wind is blowing in the right direction. We just dismiss it and think of how the apples are just perfectly ripe and ready to enjoy.

Occasionally, there will be a slight bump in the road that will juggle the apple cart a little, but soon enough everything will settle down as we continue on our merry way. Sooner or later we become less observant of the road we are traveling, and we may hit a big bump in the road. Suddenly the apple cart will be overturned and reveal that in the bottom of the pile there are rotten apples. Some are not too bad, but others are really rotten and causing others to spoil also.

We suddenly recognize that the bump in the road was a hidden blessing. Had it not happened we would have gone on as though nothing was amiss, and sooner or later our entire load of apples would have become spoiled and rotten. So, we upright the cart, wipe off and shine up the good apples, and load them back into our cart. It may not have been an easy or pleasant task, and our load is much lighter now, but we are now able to move on our way swiftly and less burdensome than before.

The bump in the road? Was that our becoming too comfortable with the way things were going, while failing to recognize the danger signs and being aware of the perils we could be facing. Was it God attempting to get our attention? Surely, the minor bumps in the road were warning signs that something may be wrong and needed our attention. Not recognizing that things were not as wonderful on the inside, as they may have appeared on the outside, allowed the rot to continue and contaminate the other apples in our load.

When one is in relationship with God, it is God who will sometimes cause that big bump in the road, that sudden change and disruption in our lives. It is not to harm us or to cause us to despair or feel defeated. It is quite the opposite! It is God's way of getting us back on track, living the life following the clear direction He has set out for us. It is God's way of helping us avoid hitting the wall of total destruction if we fail to deal with minor bumps along the way.

Just as the apples in our cart would have eventually all become rotten and unsavory or eatable, the many good aspects of our life would have eventually been influenced by the negative, thus ruining everything we had diligently strived to achieve. Sometimes one has to look and dig deeper into what is going on and root out the bad. Just as slowing down and coming to a stop in order to thoroughly go through the pile of apples in our cart, gives the opportunity to uncover and throw out the rotten apples.

Perhaps at a time when we think God is ignoring, and in fact, allowing bad things to happen to us, He is actually saving us from ourselves. It is so easy to become complacent, to let down our guard, to become greedy, jealous, and even arrogant. God knows how to cure all that. Sometimes it hurts. Then again, sometimes it results in amazing blessings we otherwise would have never had the opportunity to be a part of.

Sometimes when one finds themselves in a situation where nothing appears to be going their way and everything seems to be going against them, they may ask themselves. . .

HAS GOD ABANDONED ME?????

When we've had a dream in our heart, a plan with good intentions, a goal, an objective we strove diligently to achieve yet have failed to realize. . .

HAS GOD ABANDONED ME?????

When we have prayed, asking, asking, even begging, and telling ourselves we've tried to do all the right things and in the right ways. . .

HAS GOD ABANDONED ME?????

If we have been created by God. . .
If God truly loves us. . .
If God really cares. . .

Is Our Experience in Life A RESULT OF GOD HAVING ABANDONED US?

or,

IS IT THAT WE MAY HAVE ABANDONED GOD?

Have we turned within, deciding that we can do this on our own.
Have we closed God out of our decision-making, and decided we know what's best?
Have we stopped to even consider that perhaps God's plan is better than our plan?
Have we thought about the times in the past when God carried us through situations?
Have we praised God and thanked God for the blessings that have been bestowed upon us?
Have we considered that God has perfect timing and never comes too early or too late?
HAVE WE. . .

GOD NEVER ABANDONS US.

God always stands ready to fulfill the needs we have to live the life God has called us to live.

Perhaps. . .

We're ignoring the call of living the life God has the desire for us to live to fulfill our purpose

Could it be. . .

God's desire is for our lives to be filled with love, peace, joy, and fulfillment

not

Anxiety, grief, animosity, fear, revengefulness, greed, jealously, arrogance, and disappointment.

> "Many are the plans in a person's heart, but it is the Lord's
> purpose that prevails."
> *Proverbs 19:21 (ISV)*

Until one learns to
appreciate living without something,

they will never know how to
really appreciate
living with it.

Accepting where you are at
as being a blessing,
regardless of the situation,
is a good place to start.

SOMETIMES FATHER

Dear Lord: Sometimes we just don't know how to pray or what to pray for. Please direct our prayer, Lord.

Children: It's not that you pray, or what you pray for, it's that there should be an open line of communication between us.

I, your Lord,
know your every thought and concern. So, isn't it best, at least at times, that you just be still and listen?

I, your Lord,
have many ways in which to communicate with you. Some, you are aware of. However, at other times you may not realize it is I who is sending my message to you. Perhaps it's that sudden idea that races through your mind; that feeling of nervousness, uneasiness, unusual concern, or some other inner feeling. I may sometimes use sight or sound. I may use another person in some way or even an animal. In order to get your attention, I may even use a situation or set of circumstances. Remember children, my options are unlimited and varied.

Yes, I, your Lord,
hear and appreciate your prayers. However, don't become so wrapped up in them, trying to make them proper and right, that you fail to hear My answer. I am able to make sense of, and understand, even those thoughts and prayers that don't sometimes even make sense to you yourself.

Just remember, I, your Lord,
DO ANSWER PRAYERS, and I answer them in a TIMELY WAY, and in a way that is for your HIGHEST GOOD as well as for that of your loved ones and those whom you hold dear to your heart. So, have faith because faith is not the belief that "I will do what you want or what you may ask for." It is the belief that "I will do what is right."

SPIRITUAL LENSES

When hiking or driving through the mountains certain times in the fall, the beautiful array of colors from the changing leaves on the trees can be an awesome sight. Yet, when viewed through glasses with certain lenses, the color and beauty are even more pronounced and magnificent. It causes one to ponder the wonder of God's holy hand in having created such diverse and colorful things in nature.

Walking among the buildings in the incredible cities such as New York, Chicago, Los Angeles, Paris, or London, as well as many others, the awesome architecture of the buildings, particularly those of incredible heights, may make a person wonder how such feats are made possible. The creativity, ability, and motivation to make them a reality can be difficult to comprehend.

All one has to do to understand is put on the glasses with the spiritual lenses. Through them the image and hand of God will become evident, and it will become obvious that without the blessings and gifts God has bestowed upon mankind, none of this would be possible. God has provided the synchronicity of materials derived from nature, and in people, the imagination, ingenuity, innovation, and courage to make it happen.

When one is spiritually awakened to the awareness and presence of God in all things, it becomes obvious that mankind is, in fact, not the Creator of anything, but the co-creator in partnership with God. It is God's gifts to every person that enable them to do the things they do, whether considered routine, modest, or extraordinary.

All people have been given talents and abilities to contribute in some way, whether through occupational, entrepreneurial, benevolent, or leisure activities or hobbies, in which to thank God for these blessings in our lives. It is up to each individual to determine if they are using their God-given talents and skills to the extent God intended for them to be used.

It is a person's choice to determine the ways in which they will make contributions in the world in which they are a part. Through acknowledging and appreciating God's blessings in our lives, as we look through spiritual lenses, the answer and the choice become much clearer. Taking advantage of the opportunities God has given us to glorify Him through the application of the talents and skills we've been given, the rewards are compounded through the ways in which we are blessed.

FOR MY EYES ONLY

What God Provides for Me to See, No One Else in the Entire Universe Sees.

Having awakened early in the morning and witnessing an amazing sunrise, or in the evening gazing at an incredible sunset with no one else around, have you ever stopped to consider that you were the only individual who was seeing the sight you were blessed to see. Yes, others in some other place may have seen what you were looking at, however, not from the same location, perspective, and spiritual place you were in.

God blesses us with many things our senses are attuned to that no one else is a part of. Perhaps the smell of a beautiful flower, the antics of an animal at play, or the kindness of another person simply acknowledging our presence.

Each person is a unique creation of Almighty God. He adorns our lives with unique experiences as well. Awaken to the world around you. Embrace God's gifts of life and the beauty with which it surrounds you.

It's easy to become concerned and focus our attention on everything we perceive to be wrong, unpleasant, or just plain ugly in the world we encounter every day of our lives. Perhaps we are looking at the world with blinders on, and we can only see what is directly in front of us.

However, there is a vast array of beauty in the sights, sounds, odors, and simple experiences that we encounter every day that God has placed there for us to appreciate.

Awakened by the Spirit Within, our senses will come alive. We will experience a whole new world. We will appreciate, how, in fact, we have been blessed by God to be a part of this incredible world He has created.

THE INVISIBLE SHIELD

We may put up an invisible shield around ourselves to keep others from getting close to us. A barrier keeping others from allowing them to see the real person, or from developing a personal relationship with us. Likewise, we can build an invisible shield around ourselves that will shut God out. However, unlike others who oftentimes shun us and move on when we close them out of our lives, God is always there outside that shield.

God is always prepared to become an innermost part of our lives, provided we simply relax the shield that shuts God out by making His Holy Spirit an integral part of our lives. In fact, if we even open a small crack in that shield, God will squeeze through that tiny opening we give Him and enfold us with His love. Water will always run to a small opening and eventually leak through. God, like water, is always seeking the small opening in our hearts to enter through it and be a part of our lives.

We need only open our heart and mind to God's love for us and the many blessings He has for us. Though the people in our lives may come and go, God is always there as a friend, a companion and as an integral life line to His perfect plan for our lives.

NEED—HAVE

Believers oftentimes refer to their ability to cope with life by saying, "I need to have a relationship with God" in order to get by. It is one thing to say, "I need to have a relationship with God", another to say, "I have a relationship with God", and I am not just getting by, I am living a fulfilling and joyful life.

When we say "we need" or use the word "need", it creates the question, "Is it something we don't have, want or desire to have and want to acquire?" Words are important. Their connotation influences the mind in the way it interprets and directs action.

Need affirms wanting something not present, indicating that you want it to happen, or it may happen, indicating there also may be conditions.

"Speak words of affirmation"

"Living" affirms "Having" something in the present, it's happening now.

"I'm living this relationship I have with God", therefore, I have a relationship with God! In our mind, "Need" overrules "Have". It's just the way the tyrannical mind works. It tends to play tricks on us.

"Living" indicates something is in the present, it's happening. Is your relationship happening? Is it alive and a living part of your life? God truly favors those who live in relationship with Him. He is ever present as a friend, and as a companion.

> *"And there is a friend that stickiest closer than a brother."*
> *Proverbs 18:24 (NKJV)*

WE MIGHT HAVE IT!

It's not so important
to thank God
for what we have,
as it is to be thankful
that we have a God
who created it all,
that "we might have it"

U–RENT–IT

We are God's source of the things God needs in order to do His work here on earth. We are, in effect, God's **U—RENT—IT** outlet, His warehouse containing tools He needs to use in order to achieve the fulfillment of His agenda. Is your outlet open to lend those tools in your possession? Or, have you shuttered and locked the establishment, unwilling to let God, or anyone else for that matter, borrow and use the tools. ***Tools Which God Has Given You!*** These tools include the creativity, skills, talents, and all the abilities unique to you physically, mentally, and spiritually.

God pays very well to borrow and use your tools. He pays with His *grace* and *Favor*. In addition, God never returns the tool broken or worn out. Whatever He has used always comes back like new, better and stronger than when He borrowed it. Your tool may be well used, battered, and abused without your having taken good care of it while trying to use it for some personal objective. However, when God borrows and uses that tool to do the job He wants to use it for, when your tool is returned to you, it will be returned better than when He borrowed it. It will be cleaned, polished, strengthened, better than when new, in perfect shape, and it will be ready to be used again.

Creativity becomes more inventive, skills become broadened and honed, and we become able to do things we never anticipated or believed we could do. Even though we may have damaged our tools by self-doubt, neglect, or in some other way in which we have used or abused them, when we are open and offer them to God to be used, they are renewed and repaired through God's healing and power of restoration.

Some aspect of our lives, physical or otherwise, may be affected by a minor abrasion or possibly a major illness or catastrophe. These things are bound to happen and be part of our lives. Yet God wants us to be whole and in perfect condition and shape. That way, when we are called upon, our tool, be it a skill, talent, or unique ability, is ready for the task. Healing and being renewed are an integral part of God's plan of wholeness and health in our lives.

Open the warehouse, keep all the tools shined, in prime condition, and prepared for God to put them to use. Allow God to use the gifts He has given you to work through you to bless others; to use your hands to give comfort and strength, your heart to express love and compassion, and your mind to be creative and bring new ideas to the world. He may surprise you as to how effectively He is able to put your tool to use in service to Him.

JUST MOWING

Homeowners and those responsible for the upkeep of property approach their tasks in various ways. Whether it is "Just Mowing", edging, trimming, pulling weeds, whatever, some may consider it just a necessary evil to property ownership, or the profession or job they have chosen. Others may enjoy the task or the exercise it provides while being outside. Some just delight in working in nature, digging in the good earth, planting and nurturing plants to see them take root and grow.

No matter how a person looks at what they are doing and the way in which they approach the task, one thing they are all doing is pleasing God! Yes, pleasing God! Rather than allowing the mundane task of "Just Mowing" be nothing more than cutting a yard to keep it from getting out of hand, to please the neighbors, or keep the local officials from warning or fining you, consider instead that what you are doing is taking the gift from God and beautifying it. Why? In order to thank God for the privilege of having it in the first place.

It's not unlike a woman who uses makeup to enhance her natural beauty to make her look stunning and attractive in the presence of others, or a man who shaves or trims his beard, mustache, and hair to appear well groomed in the eyes of others. We are privileged to take the raw beauty of nature, manicure it, and transform it into a landscape of beauty.

While there are many things in nature that God has created that should never be tampered with by man, they all continue to be enhanced by His holy hand. The great mountains, forests, streams, waterfalls, lakes, and so much more are truly an awesome gift from God that man can take pleasure in by exploring in many different ways.

In order to make the world a better place in which to live, God has gifted man through man's creativity, ability, and courage to be a "co-creator" with God in designing, building, and maintaining the things we have.

"JUST MOWING"????

No, just a way to say, "Thank you God", as we enhance the appearance in glorification to God of that which He has blessed us with, this gift, the awesome earth upon which we live and exist.

"JUST MOWING"?

NO, "Just Beautifying", "Just Thanking God"

ROCK PILE

How does a rock pile become a rock pile?

One pebble at a time!

Followed by more rocks that are bigger and bigger until you have a huge,

"Rock Pile"

Opening our heart to God and having faith begins to produce small blessings. One pebble at a time!

Has God forsaken you? Do you feel abandoned and deserted by God? Have you lost faith and no longer believe? Has a prayer or request gone unanswered or unfulfilled, even though you believe you have done everything expected of you. Perhaps you have given up on God. Whatever your relationship is with God, God is still there and willing to work with you, but not necessarily on your terms. The plan God has for our lives is not negotiable. We can choose to continue to try to negotiate through whatever means we feel is appropriate and should work, or we can step back, release our lives to God, and accept His plan for our lives.

"The Catch", God knows what is in your heart. God knows the intention behind every move you make. You can't expect that by revolving your life or lifestyle by 180º, that God doesn't know that your real intention is to do a 360 as soon as you get that "Big Pile of Rocks". God is willing to work with you however. Opening our heart and releasing ourselves to God and His plan for our lives and accepting in faith that God's plan is the perfect plan will begin to produce small blessings.

God may just surprise you with one big huge "Rock Pile of Blessings." Chances are, though, that you wouldn't recognize them if He did. In time, however, you will look back and see how some little thing, a little pebble, was God showing His love for you. Then you will understand how other situations and incidents that became larger and larger filled your life with joy, love, peace, and fulfillment. Before you know it, a giving God has not just fulfilled your dreams and expectations, but greatly expanded upon them as over time they have "Piled Up" like the pile of rocks.

God's desire is to favor those who believe in Him and have faith. Sometimes that takes a lot of patience, understanding, and often, a lot of time. In the meantime, watch for those "Little Pebbles", those "Little Blessings". Don't give up on God. He never gives up on You!

"And without faith it is impossible to please Him, for whoever would draw near to God must believe that He exists and He rewards those who seek after Him."
Hebrews 11:6 (ESV)

FLAT LINED

God sees to it that everything in this world is FLAT LINED! That means that every person, while different in every respect, is on the same level as the next person. This is particularly true as it pertains to man's abilities to do what it is that God uses the skills and abilities of people to do, hands on. What one individual lacks, another is given in order to maintain the "FLAT LINE."

God's intention for us is to lean on and respect the skills and abilities of others, especially when those skills and talents complement the areas in which we lack those skills and talents. Thereby God elevates each of us, as a team so to speak, to the level "FLAT LINE", which God has set for us to achieve and maintain.

Because one person has the ability and is motivated to work with metal, another has a car to provide them with transportation. Because another has the ability and motivation to work with wood, the other has a home to live in. Etc. Etc. People who perform what some may consider menial tasks, and do them exceptionally well, are soon appreciated by those unwilling to do those tasks if they are left undone.

A park teeter-totter can't move up and down on its own. It takes two people to make it move, and according to the weight and effort of the individuals at either end, it swivels on its axis. Thereby, they have the ability, working together, to come to a point where they reach the "Flat Line" where they are proportionally and equally balanced. God's creation is one of balance. One which requires mutual cooperation to achieve a "Flat Line" of equality and achievement.

No matter one's role in life, it is necessary, in order to maintain the balance required for everything, to function as God intended. By taking pride in the contribution one makes through the talents and skills they've been blessed with by God, it is a way in which they glorify God, and demonstrate their thankfulness for the blessing of being a part of His world.

DOUBTERS???

Let them have their doubts, but as for me,
I know that there is a God, He has
been proactive
in my life!

THE SPRINTER

For a person to move forward in life, they need to have a sound footing right where they are. Accepting where one is in life, and even where they have been, which is how they have gotten to where they are, is the critical first step in moving forward.

A sprinter in running track knows two very important things as they ready themselves for the starter pistol to sound the start of a race. The first is their mental attitude. They must know in their mind and focus on; because of training, coaching, and past experiences, those in which they have won and lost, they are prepared for this next challenge. The second is getting a solid footing in the starting blocks and in their physical positioning. When the starter alerts the racers, **READY,** and the sound starting the race is heard, those first few moves, as the runner springs forward, are critical and can mean the difference between setting a new time in the record books or having a mediocre run.

In life nothing is static. Everything is evolving and changing continuously. That's the way God made it and intends for us to be involved in it. When we take into account and mentally accept where we have been and are grounded with a solid footing with where we are, we are ready to spring forward, like the sprinter, with the plan God has for our race into the future. We are prepared to raise higher and to set new records in our life, not to just finish the race, but in a way that is pleasing to God and personally fulfilling.

Faith = Confidence

The Stronger One's Faith in God, the Stronger the Faith They Will Have in Themselves.

Having the Knowledge and Belief That God Is There with You and for You Gives a Person the Confidence to Set Aside Doubt and Fear and Pursue Whatever Lies Ahead.

COLORING BOOK

Each day of our lives is like the pages of a "coloring book". There is a clear outline of what it is that it is ours to do. No matter what one's role, identity, responsibility is in life (male, female, father, mother, brother, sister, employee, employer, student, teacher, to name just a few), these are the many and varied ways in which we look at and consider ourselves and the way in which we are viewed by others. The way in which we see ourselves and the outlines by which we see and do the things we anticipate and set out to achieve are the important things to keep in mind.

Sometimes the pages go totally unaltered. Other times we may not turn the page before adding colorful highlights. Perhaps even changing a few lines to represent something totally different, when first viewed one may have perceived the page to represent. Each page offers the opportunity to take the variety of colors we have to work with and bring out the significance of every characteristic of the outline.

Every person is blessed with a measure of skills, abilities, and talents to turn an otherwise lackluster page in their life into a vibrant, consequential, and awesome page appropriate to the plan God has for their life. God already knows exactly how many pages there are in each of our "coloring books" of life. God knows the content of each page, past and present. As far as those pages we have already thumbed past, we may look back upon some and find satisfaction. Others we may have a difficult time remembering what was even on them to begin with, and yet others we may just as soon forget that they are even a page in our "coloring book".

The important pages are those we are yet to open. No matter where we are in life, no matter the responsibility, age, condition, or situation we may find ourselves in, we still have the same variety of colors to work with. In fact, with age and experience, perhaps we have many more than what we once may have had. We need not worry about how many pages may remain in our "coloring book". The page we are on is the one that is important. Even if we initially view the page with indifference and fail to see what colors we could use, or how we could use them to bring out the colorful and vibrant characteristics of the page, until the page is turned, anything is possible. That is, with God as our guide.

God gave us the colors and God knows exactly how He wants us to use them. All the blessings of life are contained in our handful(s) of colors. Turning to God in faith as we first view this new page in our life, while trusting in His love for each of us and allowing God to be a proactive part of our page of life, we will soon realize that the way in which we proceed flows without doubt or hesitation as we choose and apply the colors to our day. Thank God for every new page! Partner with God to make every page colorful and fulfilling! Praise God for the colors to make it happen!

THE GENERATOR AND THE ALTERNATOR

Until the 1960s automobiles used (DC) direct current dynamo generators with commutators.

They were replaced by (AC) alternating current generators that provided additional and more efficient electrical power because of increased electrical loads required by larger and more powerful headlamps, electric windshield wipers, rear-heated windows, and other accessories.

A direct current (DC) Generator produces and regulates the current from a vehicle's battery, which operates the vehicle's electrical system and accessories. An alternator converts mechanical energy into electrical energy through induction. The generator and alternator both produce electricity, with the primary difference between the two being that the generator cannot operate without a constant electrical source, the battery. The alternator, on the other hand, once running, produces its own electrical current without the continued need of being connected to another source, such as a battery. Once the alternator ceases to operate, however, it requires another electrical source, the battery, to start it operating again.

Our relationship with God can be much like that of both types of generators. A constant source connected to a DC generator will keep it going satisfactorily and produce a sufficient amount of energy to sustain basic accessories, but disconnected from its source of electricity, it ceases to operate. At a younger age, or at an earlier time, in our relationship with God, like the DC direct current generator we are sustained in our relationship through an ongoing connection with God. This may include regular opportunities of spiritual connectedness through family, peers, religious activities, publications, and other supportive sources. For some, though, in time, they may become more like the (AC) alternating current generator. They go along just great and are productive and confident without having that constant connectivity to God.

Then something shakes their beliefs or understanding, and sooner or later their relationship with God fades and even ceases to exist. When we fail to have the connection and an ongoing relationship with God, we may tend to cease to function effectively, and in some cases not at all. For example, when an AC generator stops working, all the electrical components as well as the vehicle itself ceases to operate.

When our spiritual life comes to a halt and unable to function, we require a powerful source to provide the spark that will "Awaken the Power of the Holy Spirit Within". God, through the Holy Spirit, is the primary source of power in our lives, just as the battery is the primary source of electrical power to start and operate a vehicle. When we remain connected by sustaining our relationship with God, like the generator and alternator of the vehicle continuously connected to the source, we will always keep functioning effectively. The DC generator may have been sufficient to operate the vehicle and its electrical accessories in the past, but today's vehicles, with more accessories, require an alternator. In today's complicated world, we also need a higher and more reliable source to keep us in relationship with God, that source is the "Holy Spirit".

God favors those who hold to this relationship and embrace His presence in their lives. God blesses those who are open to His words when He speaks to them, even when they can't hear His voice. God touches a person's life when they remain confident in Him, even though they can't touch Him. God is always there, and though a person's voice may not be heard out loud when they cry out, God hears and provides comfort and peace.

If your relationship with God has faltered or even ceased entirely, call upon Him, call His name, ask Him to "Awaken the Power of the Holy Spirit Within", He will! He wants to be your friend!

NO TILL

Years ago, a farmer would spend days preparing his fields for planting the crops by tilling the soil. After turning the soil over by plowing it to bury the stubble and weeds left from a previous harvest, the farmer would do one or more things to break up the soil in order to make it more suitable for planting seeds. He may go over the entire field with a tool called a disk, or a spike tooth drag, or one or more of several types of equipment designed for certain purposes in preparing the soil for planting. Then finally, the farmer would plant the crop with a machine specifically designed to plant the crop, be it corn, wheat, barley, or others in parallel rows with proper seed spacing. It proved to be a timely and tedious task, whether the machinery was pulled by a team of horses as it was many years ago, or by the tractors designed over the years to make the job less burdensome and time consuming.

Today, with the availability of modern and more advanced farming equipment, much of the timely land preparation is eliminated with the introduction of "No Till" (tilling) planting. Other than cutting down and chopping up stubble left from previous crops, this enormous equipment cuts into the soil, deposits seeds, fertilizer to simulate growth, and all in measured amounts and with ideal spacing. Amazingly, today's production from these new methods produces many times the amount of yield than the laborious time-consuming methods of earlier years.

One might ask themselves: Is my relationship with God like the farmer of years ago. Do I labor over trying to get it just right in my life to gain favor and blessings from God? Or do I understand that God accepts me where I am, uncultivated, covered with the stubble of life's experiences. Am I prepared and ready, below the surface, to accept God's seeds of blessings to sprout forth to glorify Him with a bountiful harvest of love and peace.

A person can concentrate on trying to do all the right things; attend church regularly, tithe, refrain from vices harmful to one's self or to others, all of which are visible above the surface. These efforts are certainly commendable and proper, yet the person may fail to open their heart to the love of God and the blessings He has the desire to plant in one's heart and soul.

Releasing one's self to God willingly and purposefully, regardless and in spite of where you are or what you have done, is like the farmer who without tedious preparation, places seeds in the ground and has faith he will reap a full harvest. Neither can a farmer just scatter the seeds around on top of the ground and expect them to grow and produce any sort of a harvest. The ground must be opened and the seed placed in the ground under all the stubble that is on the surface. Likewise, a person can't merely go through the "right moves" they believe are expected of them. They must open their heart and soul to God that He might plant the seed, and by the will of His mighty hand, manifest His blessings within.

THE LEAVES

On a beautiful early fall morning with clear skies, reacting to a light breeze, all the leaves shimmer as they sing praises to the Lord. They are thanking Him for having a wonderful year to grace the otherwise barren trees. They are telling God that they realized that it is soon approaching the season when they will wither and die. Yet, they know how blessed they are to have had the opportunity to be a small part in His wondrous world.

This leads one to be thankful to have not just one year like the leaves on the trees to have had the opportunity to be a small part in God's wondrous world, but a season to praise the Lord for His blessing's, which last all the years of a person's life.

OREO CREAM COOKIE

We're like the cream filling of an Oreo
Cream Cookie.

God is the like the cookie part of the Oreo.

God does the establishing of the events that
take place in our lives. One side of the cookie.

Then

God does the fulfilling by bringing everything
together. The other side of the cookie.

We,

the filling, must do what it is that it is ours to
do, allowing God to use us in the way He has
called us to live our lives.

Without God, we're just exposed filling without
a purpose.

Without us, God has no one to accomplish His
purpose for having created the world.

If God didn't have us, it wouldn't be an Oreo.
If we didn't have God, we simply wouldn't exist.
It would not only not be an Oreo, it wouldn't
be a world.

The world is just one Big Oreo Cookie.

MISTAKES – CONSEQUENCES

One does not learn by their "*mistakes*",
they learn from the
"*consequences*"
of their decisions
and the actions they take.

At least those "DO" who use the intelli-
gence and sound mind given them by God
to think for themselves!

The only

real challenges

we face in life

are those

we impose upon ourselves, sometimes by

our actions,

at other times

by our inaction!

DOMINOES

Domino tiles are most typically used in layout games that fall into two main categories, blocking games and scoring games. Besides playing games, however, another use of dominos is the domino show. This involves standing the dominoes on end in long lines so that when the first domino is toppled, it topples the second, which topples the third and the forth, etc., resulting in all the tiles falling. By analogy, the phenomenon of small events causing similar events leading to eventual catastrophe is what is known as the "domino effect". Arrangements from a few to millions of dominoes have been made and have taken many minutes, even hours to fall. In an event in 2005 a team set up over 4 million dominoes before toppling them over.

If you have seen one of these arrangements, you are aware that they can be simple or very complex. Built on solid and stable surfaces, the simpler arrangements may generally go in just a few directions on a flat surface. More complex arrangements are likely to run off in many different directions, climb to different heights, and even be piled upon themselves in structural forms. No two are exactly the same, and no two begin or end exactly at the same time. They all start with the toppling of a singular tile in the arrangement, and the arrangement ends with a singular tile toppling after all others have fallen.

You probably never have considered that our lives are like a domino arrangement. When God looks at each of our lives, it's as though He's looking down at dominos all set up representing every facet of our lives, including the beginning and the end. Every moment of our lives may be represented by a single domino tile. From the time we are conceived and we become one with the Spirit of God within, to when we take our last breath and our heart beats for the last time, and the Spirit within is reunited with God. For some the arrangement is uncomplicated and short, as their life is ended barely before it has begun. For others it is lengthy and extremely complicated, lasting for many years into an older age.

Before we're even conceived, God is aware of and can see every single tile, when it will topple, the direction it will fall, the next tile that will be affected and topple, and even when the very last tile will be toppled and the arrangement will cease to be. What an awesome thought to realize that God already knows every twist, turn, angle, elevation, and consequence our lives will take, like the domino arrangement, God knew before we were born how we would use the gifts and blessings He provided us with, the mistakes we would make, the ways in which we would offend Him and possibly even turn against Him, as well as the ways in which we would please Him, glorify Him, and give thanks.

The mystery of life? Maybe to us, but not to God! At this very moment, God knows what we will do in the very next, the next, and the next moment of our lives. God has already made provision, if we are in relationship with Him, to favor us and set the tiles up in a way so that they will continue to topple systemically and according to His plan. God will not allow the surface upon which the tiles are stacked to be unstable or shaken, allowing the tiles to tumble prematurely. To turn away from God however, if the surface upon which our tiles of life are stacked is unstable, their arrangement will be susceptible to being shaken by evil forces and tumble.

Turning to the Spirit of God within provides a stable surface that cannot be shaken. God already knows how the tiles will fall, because He knows the decisions and actions we will make and take. To that extent we are in control of our destiny. Yet, by releasing our lives to God, while the domino effect plays out the events in our lives will not lead to an eventual catastrophe, but rather a peaceful, rewarding, fulfilling life and the timely toppling of the tiles in our life.

LIFE THE LORD HAS ASSIGNED
Let each of you lead the life the Lord has
assigned, to which God called you.
1 Corinthians 7:17 (ESV)

When we commit ourselves to, and do our best to follow, the plan God has for our lives, God will surely bless us with love, peace, joy, and fulfillment.

When we stray form God's intended path for our lives, we become vulnerable, problems crop up, and life may become a burden and troubling.

It's like having an assigned parking space in the parking garage where we work. It may be a ways from the elevator and require a long uphill walk. Yet, because the space is in the middle of the lot, covered, between cars of friends we know and trust to be careful, we can feel confident that nothing bad will happen to our vehicle.

We could choose to go to the top of the garage, where we can be right next to the elevator and not have to walk so far. However, by doing this we may be placing our vehicle in a vulnerable place. There it would be exposed to the weather—sun, rain, hail, people walking by—and it could become damaged, or there may be other problems.

In life, sometimes we might tend to take what may appear to be the easy and short route available to us. We rationalize that nothing bad will happen and we'll get to where our tyrannical mind tells us we have a desire to be, only to find that the path we're following is bumpy, hazardous, lined with difficult decisions and challenges.

We may eventually still get to where it is that God had intended for us to go. Though, what purpose would we have served? What harm would we have caused to those we have encountered along the way? How have we inflicted pain and damage upon ourselves? In what ways have we glorified God? Has our quest been for convenience and material things rather than spiritual blessings?

It's never too late to seek God's guidance, release one's self to God, and allow God to lead you to "the life the Lord has assigned", the life "to which God called you".

It's not what you want to do through God,
It's what God wants to do through you!

SLINKY

"A toy that is a decompressed helical spring." It can perform a number of tricks, including traveling down a flight of steps end over end as it stretches and reforms itself with the aid of gravity and its own momentum.

A compressed Slinky sitting on the top step away from the edge will remain there undisturbed. That is until it is nudged close to the edge of the step and given a little push, at which point it will start traveling down those steps until it comes to rest at the bottom. It will remain there until someone picks it up and reforms it and sets it back firmly on the top step.

A person sitting on that top step of life can be like the Slinky. Everything is peaceful and uncomplicated in their life. Then something — a temptation, desire, or just curiosity put there by the tyrannical mind — may push them to the edge, and suddenly they become uncoiled and take the tumble down to that next step.

Before they know it, like the Slinky traveling down those steps, once a person gives in to evil and is pushed over the edge, things keep going down, down, down. It could be overindulgence in eating, drinking, drugs, or sex. Regardless, the gravity of the result, be it pleasure, withdrawing, escaping, avoiding life's struggles, or whatever, by its own momentum, without being stopped, the person will end up at the bottom.

Like the Slinky, at each step traveling down that flight of steps, a person may temporarily gain control and reform their life. Only to be overcome again by the temptation of evil as the tyrannical mind nudges them to the edge, where they begin to tumble down again. In many cases a person ends at the very bottom with no place to go. A place where if they are not picked up, reformed, and placed back on the top step, they will no longer have any type of meaningful existence.

Thankfully, through the "Awakening of the Power of the Holy Spirit Within" and by the Grace of God, in many cases a person never gets beyond that first or perhaps the second step. They are picked up, recoiled, and placed back at the top. Even for those who have tumbled to the bottom, who have lost all meaning in life, there is a loving, compassionate, and restoring God who will pick them up and reform their life. That tiny spark "Within", "Awakened" through calling upon the mercy of God, enlivened by the "Power" through the "Holy Spirit", will make them whole again

RAILROAD INSPECTION VEHICLE

Railroad inspection vehicles are regular trucks that ride on the rails of the tracks and have railroad car wheels that are lowered onto the rails. These allow the vehicles to be guided along the tracks with their rubber tires resting on the rail without falling off while providing acceleration and breaking. Consequently, the rubber tires and steering mechanism of the vehicle have no ability to control the direction of the vehicle other than forward and reverse. No matter how much the operator may attempt to steer the vehicle, the train wheels riding the track are in total control of the direction and destination of the vehicle.

In order to avoid an approaching train, an operator of an inspection vehicle has the ability to raise the railroad car wheels from the track in order to steer the vehicle off the main track onto a road, or redirect the vehicle onto a side track. Once the train has passed, the inspection car can return to the main line and proceed on its way. In order to avoid a collision, an inspection

Vehicle operator doesn't have an option other than to get off the main line and allow the train to pass.

It's like that with our lives. Once we've set our mind and direction on the plan God has for our lives, and we release our lives to God, no matter what the tyrannical mind tries to influence us to do, it will not succeed. It is as though, like the wheels of the train car, the Spirit within has set itself upon the rails, which follow the direction God has set for our lives.

Following and staying on the track God has laid out to direct our lives, and leaning on the Spirit of God that is indwelling to guide us on, we will nonetheless be confronted with difficulties and hazards along the way from time to time. However, unlike the inspection vehicle, we don't have to raise up in order to steer off the track to avoid an approaching challenge. With the grace of God and God's love for us, releasing our lives to follow the Spirit within, we can be safely guided along the main track and face challenges along the way and continue without being diverted from the clear direction God has for our lives.

When we are faced with challenges and the tyrannical mind does try to influence us, we do have the ability to choose to redirect our lives away from the main line where we may be faced with a confrontation. The tyrannical mind is quick to attempt to influence our lives and warn us to take the side track and avoid the oncoming challenge. If we do this at times, we may come to realize we are headed in a potentially even more hazardous direction.

At times, rather than had we faced the challenge head on, it may have become too late to avert disaster. Lost and often in despair, we may conclude that our lives would have been far different had we invoked the power of the Holy Spirit, faced the challenge head on, and forced the challenge to pass us by on the side track. An approaching train is undoubtedly a force one would be unwise to attempt to stand in the way of. However, there are times in life when we need to hold our ground and face up to the challenges we face.

Let Go of
Worry and Concern and Let God's Guidance
and Comfort Transform this
Present Challenge
into a Blessing.

THE BULL RUSH

In the "Running of the Bulls" in Spain, mayhem would happen if the bulls were in an open field somewhere and running in all different directions. As it is, their running, during the Fiestas of San Fermin in July, is through the streets of Pamplona, which directs their path between the buildings. While some people may watch from the safe distance above the streets from balconies, other more adventurous types run ahead of, alongside, and amongst the bulls, risking injury or even death from being trampled or gored.

The tyrannical mind can be like the bulls in a field. The mind can scramble in all directions on many subjects all at once. This may leave a person confused, fearful, and even paralyzed, and prevent them from being able to actually concentrate on and deal with a particular subject or matter. By abounding in hope by the power of the Holy Spirit, through awakening the power of the "Indwelling Spirit of God Within", one can quiet the tyrannical mind. In the same way the buildings bordering the streets direct the course of the bulls, the Holy Spirit will provide boundaries channeling one's thoughts in a direct coarse guided by God.

When we face situations that we find confusing or difficult, seeking guidance from the Spirit within helps to clarify what we can do that will help or make a difference. It will fortify our faith and enable us to leave it up to God in order to follow through. This peace and fulfillment come through the awareness of the Spirit of God within. By recognizing and affirming God's many blessings, in all things we will see the presence of God, the serendipity of life.

STRADDLING THE LINE

The line between being condescending and compassionate to another or their situation is very thin indeed. When we act in a way that enables others, even encourages them, to continue self-destructive actions or habits, we are being condescending. We, perhaps inadvertently, provide justification for one's actions, or at best, enforce their being and acting in marginal ways.

It is when we act in a way that discourages or finds fault with those actions that we truly are compassionate. Rather than going along with and accepting a person's behavior or actions, by stepping away we indicate disapproval, and in fact are being compassionate. We may have the desire to make recommendations or suggest certain alternate lifestyles, all of which however are only likely to be rejected and create animosity.

It is important to reflect on our personal reasons for attempting to intervene in another's situation. We may truly care for the person, have compassion for them, and want to be of influence in helping them change their life. Then again, when we are condescending, we may merely be using another's situation for self-justifications of the things we ourselves are doing. It may be self-reassuring to look at how distasteful another's actions are and be able to say to ourselves, "I'm certainly not that bad". This allows us to justify our own lack of motivation in pursuing excellence.

There are times and circumstances in our lives when it is important to use "Tough Love" in dealing with another's situation, while at the same time it may be even more important to be tough on ourselves. Doing a little soul searching and being honest with ourselves may lead us to change our own lives. This in itself may be the example our friend needs to be inspired to make the changes in their life that will benefit them.

The inner strength we have through "The Awakened Power of the Holy Spirit Within" is God's way of providing guidance in all situations in our lives. It works not only when it involves life-changing decisions in our lives, but also in the way we respond to and handle the situations we are concerned about in the lives of others. Yes, God desires that we show compassion for others and their circumstances. It's not easy at times to know what to do, how and when to do it, or even if we should do anything at all.

> "GOD DOES NOT WANT EASY,
> GOD WANTS SINCERE,
> BEING SINCERE IS NOT ALWAYS EASY"

THE PEACOCK
AND
ITS FLUME OF FEATHERS

Every single day, God is starting something new in your life. After all, He is the establisher. Whatever it may be, it may not be obvious. We may have no idea what it is, or even realize that it's actually happening. Even if we did acknowledge that something new was happening, we likely would be confused by it. For that matter, we'd probably have no idea the role it plays in the plan God has for our life today, tomorrow, and beyond.

The amazing thing is that God already has a myriad of things He is orchestrating in our lives. In addition to this new thing He is doing, there are things that are continuously being carried out that are in various forms and in various stages of development.

It's like the peacock strutting along with its feathers neatly tucked in, not making it look obvious as to what is there and its potential beauty. But when the peacock crows with the feathers closely cropped, it's a call for those around to pay attention. When the feathers fan out and are exposed, all the tail feathers of the peacock are raised up into a beautiful fan and display of colors.

So, too, with what God is doing in our lives. We can't see everything that is there, what is happening, or how beautifully everything is working together. However, if God spoke out and displayed for us to see all the wonder and beauty of everything He is doing in our lives, we would be amazed!

THE MASTER ARCHITECT

God created this world in such a way that all living things, in some way, contribute to the evolution and the changes that occur.

God is the master architect and enabler of everything that takes place.

Whether it's the ever-changing shape of the earth with its magnificent mountains, valleys, streams, waterfalls, lakes, and oceans; whether it's with the nourishment it takes for plant life and trees to grow, or the instinct of an animal to seek self-preservation; or whether it's the abilities, skills, creativity, and the dreams God places in the hearts, minds, and bodies of man.

God, through and by using these gifts He has bestowed upon man, builds, creates, and applies those blessings to provide food, shelter, and things of convenience.

It is everything interlaced together that result in the evolution, as God has planned it, and keeps His mighty hands upon. If it is God's will, it will be nurtured and grow; if not, it will simply wither and die.

PACE YOURSELF

To be a successful long-distance runner, the athlete learns how to pace them self. In order to finish the entire coarse, it is imperative to conserve energy to sustain themselves to be able to complete the final stages and finish the race.

Expending large amounts of energy in the early stages of a long run may prevent the runner from having the sustaining energy and stamina needed towards the end to finish, or even have that extra push it may take to win the race.

Sudden bursts of speed during the race may steel the required physical resources to endure to the end. Remaining consistent and resisting the urge to speed up, particularly when others may be passing you, gives you the extra stamina to continue, eventually even passing those who surged past you only to deplete their energy and ability to continue to the end.

In life we are somewhat like the runner in a long-distance race. We can move steadily along the path God has set for our life and avoid chasing after one thing after another in somewhat of a frenzy. When we accept that God's plan for our lives is a consistent and orderly plan for our daily lives, and when we have faith by "Awakening the Power of the Holy Spirit Within", we will trust God's plan and timing. We will instinctively know and be guided in doing the things that it is for us to do. We will not be tempted to jump at every situation that appears to be attractive or interesting.

God's Spirit helps us to pace ourselves, the way the runners pace themselves, in order to achieve those things God has for us to do in fulfilling His plan for our lives here on this earth.

In a like manner, we must use the gifts and talents that have been given to us by God in order to fulfill His plan for our lives in a resourceful way. Being jealous and envious of the talents, skills, and accomplishments of others, and trying to be someone we aren't meant and created by God to be, only drives us to break the pace God has set for our lives.

God has a divine plan for us. God gives us everything we could conceivably need to fulfill that plan, and God gives us the exact amount of time in which to complete that plan, be it a few years or many.

When we decide to start chasing the ways, accomplishments, and worldly accumulations that others have, we risk breaking the perfect stride God has for our lives. We risk our happiness, health, relationships, and even our very lives just because someone has passed us up. As life unfolds however, living in faith that the "Awakening of the Power of the Holy Spirit Within" is our perfect guide, and having done our best to maintain the pace God set for us, we will prevail and finish the race as a winner, while others have fallen by the wayside.

Once you have done all you can do. . .

STAND STILL

REMAIN CALM

BE CONFIDENT

GOD WILL SEE YOU THROUGH!

GOD IS OUR VINDICATOR

God knows the truth about every situation in our lives. God knows when we have been taken advantage of or used in an unjust, unfair, and abusive way. Even when we don't recognize the truth of a situation or the warning signs, God does. God is our vindicator. God is a restoring God. Whatever has caused us harm, God will make up to us abundantly. God knows that the ungodly prey upon those who may be vulnerable.

Yet, God also knows those who are willing to serve by helping others. God does not overlook these kind deeds.

Nor does God fail to recognize the truth about those who perhaps are the recipients of acts of kindness they didn't justly deserve.

God is a just God, God Is Our Vindicator!

GETTING TRACTION

In climates where people are likely to encounter heavy snow and icy roads, many times it is necessary to equip their vehicles with special tires and even special chains in order to navigate the harsh elements. Otherwise they may find themselves stuck, and without having any traction, all the wheels of the vehicle will do is just spin the tires, failing to move the vehicle in any direction. The inventive individual may come up with ways to get the wheels to move in order to get traction. Spreading things such as sand, salt, and even kitty litter in front of and under the wheels will sometimes provide enough traction to get the vehicle unstuck and moving. In certain situations, a few helping hands to push, or having another vehicle to help, will get it done. As a last resort, they may have to call for the assistance of a tow truck. There are certain parts of the world where winter climates can be so challenging that in certain areas and on certain roads, a specific type of tire, snow tire, or chains are legally required.

We can sometimes find ourselves getting stuck where we're at in life. Somehow, we have lost traction and are standing still, unable to move on our own without some kind of assistance. In times like this, it may only take an inventive thought, which we are inspired by through prayer. Other times it may require a more in-depth period of meditation to regain the traction to get our day or a certain project moving again. Then there are the times that on our own, we just can't seem to get going, and it takes an encouraging word or suggestion of another person to help us regain our traction and proceed. How about those times we become so stuck that no matter what we do or what some other person says or does, we just remain stuck, spinning our wheels going positively nowhere. That is when it's necessary to call for assistance. That is when we need to call upon God through the Holy Spirit to pull us up and out of our dilemma.

Just as an operator is standing by to dispatch a tow truck that is always there to answer the call of a stranded motorist, God is standing by to dispatch the Holy Spirit to answer the call of a stranded soul. But why wait until the emergency arrives? Like a motorist will equip themselves with special equipment, we are able to equip ourselves with the special equipment God provides through our making His Holy Spirit an ever-present part of our lives. How? First of all, by recognizing the role God is already playing in our lives by blessing us with life, spirituality, health, and welfare. Second, by simply appreciating the world around us and its awesomeness, and being ever mindful of the serendipitous events that occur in our lives all by the hand of God. Then, remembering to constantly thank God for His presence, goodness, and the love He sheds upon us. Getting Traction? Staying connected with God through His Holy Spirit within, you may slip from time to time, but God will see to it that you never get stuck or stranded.

TWEAKED

Has God just tweaked me? Has my life been changed in some slight way in order to improve it? Has there been a small adjustment in fine-tuning my life?

God has a plan for each of our lives. When we're in tune with that plan and release ourselves to God so that He might guide us along our way, unexpected tweaking may occur from time to time.

In this world, it is not unusual for our tyrannical mind, or the tyrannical minds of others, to entice us to stray from God's plan for us.

Having been blessed with the Holy Spirit within, God will make the adjustments in our life to suppress the influence of tyrannical minds. God is totally aware of consequences, even though we sometimes fail to acknowledge them ourselves. We may rationalize, but God doesn't. We may make excuses, but with God, there are none.

Yet God is merciful, compassionate, and loving, and He desires that we live a life that is fulfilling, without strife and filled with love and peace. Yes, our loving God may tweak our lives from time to time. It may take us by surprise. We may find it confusing and even uncomfortable. It may seem wrong at the time and unfair.

Once we realize we've been tweaked, it's important to look back upon our lives and perhaps the times God has tweaked our lives in a way that has truly turned out to be a blessing. That is our wonderful, loving Creator. The one who not only breathed life into us, but set forth a plan for our lives, and is the steward of that plan.

Praise God!

If you don't have faith in yourself or your ability to do a certain thing . . .

Perhaps the question you should be asking is . . .

Do you have faith in God?

With God all things are possible!

AIRPLANE VS. AMPHIBIOUS AIRCRAFT
(seaplanes–floatplanes)

There are three basic criteria that must be taken into account for an airplane to become airborne. One is its weight, another the power of the engine, and the third is the wind resistance. Of course, the training and skill of the pilot are also important, as well as other mechanical and environmental circumstances.

An amphibious aircraft, however, has one additional factor that must be considered, and it is critical to its ability to lift off the water. That is the drag resistance the water creates, which tends to make it more difficult to become airborne. Typically, the pilot must start the assent by gaining a sufficient amount of speed so that the flotation devices begin to skim along the top of the water, then liftoff is possible and it is enabled to become airborne. While an aircraft is able to become airborne from a runway in a reasonably short distance, the amphibious aircraft requires a much longer stretch of water before it is able to become airborne.

When we are aligned with God through the "Awakened Power of the Holy Spirit Within", we are able to break loose of the earthly bounds, like the airplane, and soar to new heights in our relationship with God and in fulfilling His purpose for our lives. However, when we aren't in alignment with God's plan for our lives, we drag our feet. Then when God wants us to get going, we are more like the amphibious aircraft. We may eventually see the light and heed signs of discord, but it can be a long stretch that we must transverse in order to get back to our relationship with God.

God's plan for each of us is to give us the lift to reach new heights in our relationship with Him and in the way we live our lives. Even when we become bogged down by circumstances in our lives and in the world around us, God knows how to get us up to speed so we can break free of the resistance that we are faced with. In the way the pilot must take additional steps to free the amphibious aircraft from the drag of the water, we must take the additional step of having the initiative to call upon God to "Awaken the Power of the Holy Spirit Within" in order that we are able to break free.

BOOSTER ROCKET

God blesses us with many talents, skills, and abilities. These are the tools we are given to follow the path God has for our lives. Generally, in the normal course of living, these tools are adequate to meet the needs of accomplishing the tasks in life in order to flourish.

At times, however, we are faced with a situation that may appear beyond our ability to handle or even cope with. It may be personal, such as a health challenge, relationship issue, or a financial problem. It could also be a situation involving a loved one or close associate. At the inception of being aware of the challenge, we may feel helpless or defeated and tempted to relinquish any attempt to deal with it. That is when God steps in with the supernatural gifts of wisdom and strength to get us through, to pull us up, and to help us over the hurdle we are faced with.

It's much like sending a space vehicle into outer space. A powerful rocket lifts the vessel from the ground high into the atmosphere. However, without a booster rocket it would fall short of escaping the gravity of earth's pull and fall back to the surface of the earth. The booster rockets of a space vehicle not only give it the extra momentum to reach outer space, but they allow it to maneuver while in outer space and adjust its trajectory in order to return to earth at the right time and in exactly the right place in which it is supposed to land.

In like manner, God's supernatural gifts not only lift us above the ability we have to achieve on our own, they enable us to maneuver our way around the difficult times we are facing and return to the normalcy of life we are destined by God to be a part of. When we live with an "Awakened Power of the Holy Spirit Within", we are automatically connected to the supernatural power of God. In a moment when we require that little extra, and even that extraordinary push, to meet life's challenges, we will experience the power of God, The Holy Spirit, proactively involved in our lives.

However, our tyrannical mind *WANTS "IT" NOW,*

E V E R Y T H I N G!!!!!!!!!

Do we really want the things we think we need to follow the path we're taking, in order to get what our tyrannical mind dictates or tries to convenience us that we desire?

Or . . .

do we honestly want the things that will fulfill the dreams God has placed in our hearts, the things we truly need to follow the clear direction God Has for our lives?

God truly has in the past, is now, or in the future will give us exactly everything we need to realize the dreams He has placed in our hearts.

It's the impatience stirred up by the tyrannical mind that makes us anxious, doubt, and even question if God is truly there and providing those things we need. The fact likely is that God is already giving us those very things every day.

So instead of giving in to the tyrannical mind, awakening and calling upon the Spirit within will help us to realize, appreciate, and accomplish these things. Today and each day that piece, or those pieces, in the puzzle will come into focus to complete the picture God has for our lives.

So, bring to fruition the dreams God places in your heart. Be strong, let your heart take courage, and wait patiently for the Lord. Oftentimes, the answer to your prayers and the fulfillment of the dreams in your heart will come as you stand back and allow the unfolding of God's perfect and divine order take place.

WHO WOULD YOU HIRE FOR THE JOB?

Have you ever asked yourself; if you were to hire the perfect person to make something for you that needed to be intricate in design, flawless in construction, and the person you hired would be willing to stand behind their work completely, who would you hire?

I'd hire God!

God designed the universe and everything in it, with each infinitesimal complexity and detail intertwined in a way that everything could work in concert together and yet function independently.

Then, **God created** the universe and everything in it to perfection. In its inception, to the last detail, everything worked and performed exactly the way it was intended.

Best of all, however, **God provided** His creation with an infinite guarantee. If anything, at any time, should go wrong with it, you can go directly to the head of the organization to ask for help in resolving the situation.

Now stop and consider the entirety of the situation. God created everything, each person, every creature in the universe, the good earth and everything that is part of it, all the galaxies in the universe, everything, and created it from a vast void, from nothing.

At the inception everything started out okay, but in time things started to break down, and not everything was working quite according to His plan. So, what did He do? He didn't turn His back on the whole thing and say, "O' well"! He sent a "fix-it man" as His personal representative to oversee setting everything right and moving in the proper direction.

In fact, His personal "Fix-It-Man", Jesus, gave His entire lifetime to not only demonstrating how this whole thing was intended to work, but to do things of a miraculous nature to heal, mend, fix, direct, and even personally demonstrate the epitome of commitment and self-sacrifice in His willingness to help straighten things out. He gave the ultimate gift, His Life, in order that we would be aware of God's desire to see that everything works according to the way He had intended.

And as if that wasn't enough to help us get things straight, God made each of us temples of the Holy Spirit. God instilled in each of us His Holy Spirit to be there to direct us every time we turned to Him in despair when something stopped functioning as it should. (not unlike having a computer chip inserted under the skin upon which everything of importance in our lives is immediately available to those in need of the information).

Yes, I believe the one I want to hire is God Himself, because I know I can go directly to Him when things break down. Best of all, He always has the perfect answer. He is the healer, the restorer, the miracle worker, and there is no time limit as to when His guarantee will run out. Not in 1 year, 100,000 miles, or ever, because whatever it is that breaks down, it has an everlasting guarantee and it is foolproof.

It's like the saying, "It's not the machine that has a problem, it's the operator". God, my machine has a problem here and there, and I know it's not the equipment, but how I operate it. Will you help me get it going again the way it's supposed to be going?

OPPOSING VIEWPOINTS

People in one part of the world praising God

for a new day that is dawning,

People in another part of the world
praising God

for a day that is drawing to conclusion.

However, both feeling blessed to be a part of
this magnificent world, God's creation, upon
which we are blessed to be "Instruments of
His Love and Peace"!

CHANGING THE PAST

Has the question ever came to mind, ever while praying and meditating, if God can in fact do anything, couldn't He change the past? Why can't we go back and have God change the past? Couldn't He make all the wrongs right and the memories about difficult times less burdensome?

Then, the thought might have occurred to you — He probably can. However, do you really want God to change things? As one looks at individual situations, one may ponder how they might have been different. Perhaps according to how one thought they should have occurred at that time, or how one may have had the desire for a situation to have taken place at the time. Think about how things did turn out and then consider how they may have turned out. The fact is things could have been much worse and more detrimental than they actually turned out to be. In fact, in many situations there was a gold lining and an unexpected positive side.

So, it may be wise to conclude, while God may choose not to go back to change things, He can **alter the future**. God lets go of the past. It's happened, done, and nothing can be done to change it. But with the grace of God helping us to set aside the past, He will guide us in altering the future in a way that the past is incidental to where we are now, and with what the future in our lives is to be.

God has a unique way of using what has happened in our lives in the past to bless us in the future. God can turn what the enemy meant for evil and use it to our advantage. It's our responsibility to let go, release the past, accept where we are at, and trust and have faith in God that He will oversee our future. We must first however, do what it is that it is ours to do. Accept that God has a plan for our lives, and it's a plan for good and for blessings. Acknowledge that God provides us with every conceivable thing we need in order to follow that plan. As we release ourselves to God, we are free of the opinions of man, released of the past, and awakened to the Power of the Spirit of God Within. It's not about where we've been, it's all about where we're going!

MY DISAPPOINTING GOD

I look back at my lifelong experience of being disappointed by God, in that He has never given me what I prayed for.

Not that I wasn't blessed with a good life, and generally with things and situations that made up for and turned out to be better than I had prayed for in the first place.

However, the amazing thing is, when I stopped praying for stuff, certain outcomes, personal desires, and simply left it up to God to fulfill my needs — wouldn't you know — God began to fill my needs and desires with more and better than I would have actually asked for.

Sometimes we limit God and put God in a box by trying to tell God what we need and what would make us happy. Rather than trusting and having faith in the fact that God really does understand and know what is the most fulfilling and rewarding way for us to live our lives.

God is the **ESTABLISHER**, having ***supernatural knowledge***, thereby He knows every little detail of what we need to fulfill the plan He has for our life. God is the **FULFILLER,** having the ***supernatural power*** with which to accomplish the plan He has for our life. It is up to us to release ourselves to the will of God and not be burdened by the tyrannical dictates of greed, jealousy, and arrogance.

MY PRAYER:

Dear God, you have disappointed me and let me down time and time again, so with my sincerest appreciation, thank you!

God has put dreams in our hearts and they coincide with

THE CLEAR DIRECTION GOD HAS FOR OUR LIVES.

TURBO CHARGER

(Super Charger)

When a super charger is added to a vehicle's engine, it force-feeds the engine with petroleum and air in order to provide additional power. Typically, they are used on more powerful engines, such as in racing vehicles. The engine operates normally until the turbo charger begins to operate, (kicks in) thereby increasing the torque and potential speed of acceleration. Some of today's modern cars and vehicles are equipped with one of these devices simply to provide additional power to a smaller engine to meet routine driving conditions.

In our lives things can be going along just fine, and we can feel confident and at ease with where we are. We go about routine tasks somewhat effort-lessly. We may have no desire to step outside of our comfort zone. We accept where we are and rationalize it is likely where we're going to stay and where we belong. Life is good! Our relationship with God is good as well, we have faith and try to live a decent life, and it's that faith in God that keeps us going. Just like a vehicle with the smaller engine, we do just fine getting around in order to meet routine demands.

Is that what God wants for us? Perhaps! Or maybe God has something far more important to do with and in our lives. Could it be that God's plan, if we release ourselves to Him, will be to use us to fulfill something far greater than what we could ever imagine ourselves. "Awakening the Power of the Holy Spirit Within" is like the turbo charger kicking in on a racing engine. God's plan may be to take us farther, faster, and more powerfully than we could ever do on our own.

Each of us from conception is equipped with the Holy Spirit, the turbo charger. It is permanently installed and ready to "Kick In" as the need presents itself. It is up to us to determine if we are like the small engine, with just enough assistance from God, the Holy Spirit, to just get along and simply make it through life. Or, are we willing to be a more powerful engine fitted with and using the turbo charger, allowing God to kick in the Holy Spirit in our lives to propel us supernaturally and effortlessly along life's journey to greater accomplishments in His Name and to His Glory.

CHOICES

God *Does Not* Make Choices for Us, However, God *Does Know* the Choices We Will Make

Consequently, God provides for us everything we need to travel the clear path He has for our lives. However, because He knows the choices we will make and how we may stray from the clear path He has for our lives, He has even made provisions for these times in our lives.

When we enter this world, it's as if God has prepared a suitcase with everything in it that we will need for our journey on this earth. This includes literally everything; every talent, every skill, every relationship whether it be family, friend or spouse, every opportunity, every emotional and spiritual need, every materialistic need, even one's desire for love, the need for healing of heart, mind, body, and soul. The list of these blessings is literally unending.

Continuing that analogy, as we sort through the contents of the suitcase, sometimes we may not find what it is that we think we need at a particular time. However, be assured that God has placed everything there that we could possibly need. Perhaps we have overlooked it, or just didn't recognize it for what it really was or was intended for. Or, maybe God has placed it in a hidden compartment in our suitcase only to be found at the right time and place for the right purpose. It surely is there, and if not, perhaps that is God's way of preventing us from going down a path leading to disaster or straying too far from the clear path He Has for Our Life. *"God Does Not Make Choices for Us, However, God Does Know the Choices We Will Make"*, and more importantly God knows the consequences of every choice we make.

God, with his infinite wisdom, unlimited power, perfect timing, and love for His children, will never, never let us make a choice where He isn't able to turn what may be evil and use it to His advantage and to our benefit for good.

Pointed PS:
More importantly, our God, with His perfect timing and love for His children, will never, never let us overlook the right person with whom we are to walk down that clear path He Has for each of our lives.

ANTI-VIRUS

The brain is like the hard drive of a computer. It contains everything that has ever been entered into the computer.

The mind acts as the operating system, the software, that accesses the brain to utilize the information required at any given time in order to effect a given function one wishes the computer to perform.

The human body is the instrument that carries out the function that the mind directs us to do and the brain says we are capable of doing.

So, why do we need God? Because without God there would be no brain, mind, or body with which to carry out His plans, through each of us, for this world.

If an IT (Information Technologist) would open one's hard drive so everything in it could be revealed, we would likely ask where a large majority of the information came from. We wouldn't remember anything about how or where much of it came from. It is obvious that some of the information we put there ourselves. However, a lot comes from other sources, such as software programs, apps, social media, and more. Many of those that come from other sources are beneficial and assist the operating system to function somewhat more efficiently and faster. Others may be detrimental, such as viruses that can slow down or even crash the hard drive and cause a computer to not even start up. Fortunately, there are anti-virus programs that a person can install and use to remove these potentially devastating enemies that attack our computers and hard drives.

So also with the brain, we have an amazing capacity in the brain for storing information. Some comes through our personal exposure to life experiences, study, and circumstances. The rest is the gift God has blessed us with, the supernatural power of ideas and information. Some information, for which we are responsible for storing in the brain can certainly be beneficial, yet other information can be detrimental.

The tyrannical mind can open the way for a virus to infiltrate the brain and be a negative influence in our lives. It will raise doubt, fear, slow us down, and possibly even bring us to a complete halt. Viruses emerge from the evils of greed, jealousy, arrogance, and revengefulness. Some we bring upon ourselves with thoughts, desires, and actions. Others come from the tyrannical minds and actions of others.

God, through the Holy Spirit within, is the anti-virus for the brain. By "Awakening the Power of the Holy Spirit Within", we raise the level of resistance and suppress the influence the tyrannical mind tries to hold over our actions. Excessiveness in eating, drinking, sexuality, and other behavioral traits are all "strengths" supported by the tyrannical mind. "Awakening the Power of the Holy Spirit Within" allows a person the strength to overcome and reduce or eliminate the power and grasp of the tyrannical mind. This then integrates a defense in the brain so that when the tyrannical mind attempts to test a person's resolve, the feedback from the brain to the mind resonates with the information that supports self-control, moderation, and even change.

Like the information in a hard drive we are unaware of, there is information God has instilled in the brain that we are also unaware of, until we need to call upon it to guide us on a path in life that is pleasing to Him. A path of peace, joy, love, fulfillment, and wholeness.

FINAL SCORE

Many people follow and appreciate sports of all kinds, whether it's a team or an individual competitor. The fan cheers them on to victory, sometimes passionately. In many situations, victory or defeat comes down to the final actions or waning seconds in the competition before the final score determines the winner.

The action leading up to the final score can appear to be great or perhaps even questionable, appreciated or criticized, that all depends on how the fan's competitor is doing in their opinion, and from their particular viewpoint. Ultimately, the final score may be cause for celebration or disappointment. Everything may appear to be going in the direction the fan approves of, or otherwise is unhappy with. Then, in the final moments, as the result of a sudden move by one of the competitors, everything changes, which results in the "Final Score".

Life itself can be very similar with many ups and downs, give-and-takes. Sometimes life situations call for celebration, other times disappointment. A situation may be moving along in a smooth and expected way, and suddenly everything changes and disaster appears imminent. Another life experience may have all the signs of being disappointing and even harmful, when some little thing happens that reverses the situation and brings about a positive or inconsequential result.

No matter, because when one is in relationship with God, attuned to the power of the Holy Spirit within, every situation, every challenge, every encounter will prove in the end to be to one's advantage. With God in control the "Final Score" is the winning score, the perfect score, the end result that will raise a person to their highest good. God knows how and what it will take to be a winner, and consequently, make a person in relationship with Him a winner in the process.

LET THE MAN DO HIS JOB!

When I have something that is fairly technical that is in need of repair or service, such as a TV, computer, electrical appliance, or even my car, I would call a certified professional to do the job. (something I should probably do even if the repairs aren't technical) I would rely on a technician with training, knowledge, and the proper tools to repair the item properly. It wouldn't do me any good to try to tell the person how to do the job, or even be looking over the person's shoulder hoping to learn how to fix it myself the next time. Even if I thought I could do the repair work myself, it isn't likely that I would have the right tools, adjust things to the right tolerance, and so on. The times I have tackled that type of thing, I have nearly always ended making it worse. It ended up costing me even more to get the thing right than if I had called for the proper technician in the first place.

So it is with our lives and sometimes with the lives of others. We sometimes mess around trying our own quick fix, or meddle in the affairs of someone else and just end up messing things up even more. If we had consulted the True Professional, the Master Fixer, the Great Healer and Miracle Worker, God, things likely would have been a lot different. Besides, God is on call 24/7/365, and His rates never change regardless if it's a weekend or holiday. Actually, all you have to do is ask. Now that's a reasonable rate to pay for a perfect solution. Of course, we'll only muddle things up if we try to help or try to be part of the solution, if we are not directed to take an active part. So why not "JUST LET GO AND LET GOD". After all, He does know the perfect solution and has the absolute ideal timing. We wouldn't try to tell a serviceman how to fix a computer when we know nothing about its internal workings. So why try to tell God how to fix something when many times we don't even know how we got there in the first place.

So "LET GO AND LET GOD",
because God guarantees His work.

KALEIDOSCOPE

When we think about the way in which God has blessed us, we generally focus in on a particular event or situation. It may be something that is currently happening or has just recently happened. Sometimes something will happen that will bring to mind an unusual or even seemingly supernatural occurrence or event. There are times that this singular situation or event may lead to additional thoughts of blessings in other areas of our lives as well. To be sure, that is a way to give glory to God, a way of praising God for having done something special in our lives, or in that of others we care about.

Wouldn't it be awesome however, if we could visualize all the blessings that God has favored us with throughout our lives? Perhaps we can! If you have ever been intrigued when looking through a kaleidoscope,[1] you will be familiar with the colorful patterns and intricate designs that it creates — a seemingly unending variety of colors and patterns never appearing to repeat one another no matter how long a person peers into the instrument. Closing one's eyes, allowing the brain to project a visualization of past blessings to reflect in the mirror of your mind can be similar to the experience of that of a kaleidoscope. As images begin to flash by, one incident will lead to another and another. Blessings we have long forgotten will suddenly appear with others, which are perhaps similar or more recent. Pleasant memories visualizing how God was there in our most pressing times, in our most pleasurable times, and in times we least expected to be blessed.

Many times we fail to recognize that some major event, or even some little thing that may have happened, was a result of a proactive God being involved in our lives. We take for granted that what happened was fate, inevitable, or just a normal development. When we strive to live our lives in accordance with God's plan, God is continuously blessing us. It's important to realize that a particular experience is truly a blessing that God has bestowed upon us. God knows our every thought, desire, and need, and prepares our way by establishing those things that are necessary to fulfill His plan.

They may not always completely correspond with those things we believe are in our destiny, but we can be assured that the plan God has for our lives is better than anything we ever could imagine ourselves. Looking at our past blessings as though looking through a kaleidoscope underscores our faith and trust that God's plan is a path to future blessings.

[1] A kaleidoscope is an optical instrument, typically a cylinder with mirrors containing loose, colored objects such as beads or pebbles and bits of glass. As the viewer looks in to one end, light entering the other end creates a colorful pattern, due to repeated reflection in the mirror.

An alternate version of the instrument omits the object cell and allows the observer to view any scene through it, in the manner of a telescope. This version of the instrument can transform a portion of any scene into an abstract repeating mosaic

AUTUMN LEAVES

Consider yourself as being a large, fascinating, and beautiful leaf, aglow from the stroke of God's brush with the colors from His pallet of moisture, temperature, and love floating through the air being carried by the wind. Sometimes, you land on the ground among other leaves that are scattered about, each showing the uniqueness of God's artistic expression. Then, gently picked up again by the wind, you float and dance on to another scattering of colorful leaves. At times you may land in a pile of closely hovering leaves, desperately resisting being blown about with uncertainty as to where they will end up.

As you reflect on your predicament, you can see that you may have been one of those leaves that clung tightly to the tree, stubbornly holding tight and refusing to let go. However, sooner or later you would have gently lost your grip and gracefully floated to the ground. There, every bit of nutrient would have been drained from you as you sunk deep into the ground, adding nourishment and vitality. This having been the inevitable to which you would have contributed in providing a new cycle of growth to take place in a new season, fulfilling your destiny.

Yet, in your predicament floating from place to place and pile to pile, it's apparent that at some point you're going to end up in one of those piles, far from where you began, embracing a closely knit group of leaves. As a part of this consortium of leaves originating from many different trees, you can see that each is unique unto itself, only as God could have predetermined and masterfully stroked with His brush and pallet of colors. But what will become of this diverse combination of God's creations?

Will you be in a pile that in combination will be reborn in a highly nutrient form to eventually be scattered about contributing to significant numbers of diverse, beautiful, and colorful flowers that will bring delight and pleasure? Or, will you give vitality and provide an abundance of food that will provide life and sustenance to many? On the other hand, will you end up in a pile that will be swept away to be burnt and destroyed? Will your pile be reduced to a hand full of ashes, with depleted nutrients unable to provide any sustenance? Will the pile you are a part of be self-defeating and destructive, all consumed with self-interest and importance?

Pray that God has blessed you to be free to float from the safety and sureness of your beginnings, that you might in some way ultimately land in and be a part of contributing to a pile that will stimulate new growth, vitality, and glorify the artist who lovingly had shone His light upon them.

BLACK ICE

Life is generally like driving a car. We are confident, hands are on the wheel directing the vehicle in the direction we want it to go, at a speed we are comfortable in traveling, going along without a concern or doubt that we'll reach our destination. Just as we may have confidence in the direction and pace our life is moving. However, in colder regions ice can form on certain areas of the roadway and not on others, particularly on bridges. This ice is referred to as black ice because it's difficult, if not impossible, to see or realize it's there until you're on it.

On a cold wintery day, one can suddenly hit a patch of the black ice on the road. The road may have been clear and dry, things were going along perfectly, then suddenly, without warning, you realize you are on a patch of black ice and have no control over the direction of the vehicle, and are helpless to anything about it.

However, if you've maintained the car well, have good tires and don't panic, the car will most likely continue on its coarse without a problem, and soon you'll be back on dry pavement and back in total control of the vehicle. However, when you hit that black ice, if the car is not maintained well, has tires with major tread wear, and if you panic and try to take control steering erratically or accelerating or breaking too abruptly, the likelihood is that the car will spin out of control and cause an accident or veer off the road and end up over an embankment and cause a major problem.

Life is generally much like that also. We set our sights and goals on a given course, make all the right moves to proceed in the direction we choose to go, and travel along in life without a worry or concern. But then something unforeseen occurs and blindsides us, whereby we suddenly appear to have lost control. Under these circumstances we may panic, try to take measures to resolve the situation, only to overcorrect and cause a bad situation to become a more tragic disaster.

Just as we must maintain our vehicles in order to be prepared for unexpected bumps or black ice on the road, in our lives we must prepare ourselves for unexpected circumstances that may come up from time to time. We do this by making God an ever-present part of our lives — a Guardian who will effortlessly guide us through any challenge that we are faced with in life, even when unanticipated or unexpected. Allowing the Spirit within to be the everlasting light that guides us, we will continue on a steady path regardless of obstacles we may encounter.

BLESSINGS / SNOWBALL

God's blessings are like a snowball rolling downhill.

They just get bigger and bigger as they role on.

With and through faith, it is for us to form an alliance with the Holy Spirit acknowledging God's love for us and God's desire to bless us abundantly.

Just as a snowball grows larger and larger as it rolls along, God's blessings become greater and greater as we proceed along God's path for our lives.

A little snowball, now a giant ball of hard-packed snow and ice, can blast through the hardest barriers as it descends hurtling itself through obstacles in its path.

Likewise, with the blessings of God, the Holy Spirit within, we are able to overcome obstacles and difficulties in our path.

While at times we may appear to be slowed down, hesitant, or stopped, God is blessing us and seeing us through.

With God all things are possible, and He will not allow anything to stand in our way as we follow the direct path He has for our lives.

My Mouth

(through the written word)

Shall Speak Wisdom;

the Meditation of the Heart

Shall Be Understanding

Psalm 49:3 (RSV)

SNOWFLAKES

On a cold wintery day, as snow gently falls from the sky, one might reflect on how each snowflake is uniquely shaped by God. Some flakes glide softly to the ground, providing a blanket of protection and undisturbed beauty to grassy areas. Others float lightly onto trees and shrubs, glistening like ornaments. Then others land on the pavement, sidewalks, rooftops, and an assortment of other places where they neither glisten or stand out, nor do they remain protected and undisturbed. Regardless of where any of them may land, their tenure in time is measured by the conditions they encounter.

Each individual who enters this world is also uniquely shaped by God. Some live lives that are somewhat uneventful. Through family, friends, occupation, and the application of their skills and talents, they contribute to the world around them during their tenure on earth, somewhat like the snowflakes that glide softly to the ground providing a blanket of protection and undisturbed beauty. Others live a life of glamor as an elite. Like the sown flakes that float lightly onto trees and shrubs glistening like ornaments, they tend to be aloof and above the norm, attracting attention while being aggressive and perhaps even intimidating. Then there are those that are more erratic and move all about, at times being blown and pushed around, stamped upon and shoved out of the way. Other times they cause complications and trouble for everything and everyone around them.

How does one perceive themselves? Is it the way in which they assume how others see them, or perhaps in the way they want others to see them! One's manner and their behavior is greatly influenced by this perception, whether accurate, imagined, or even idealized. Regardless, like the snowflake, everyone's tenure here on earth is measured. For snowflakes, it is dependent primarily upon conditions. For people, the conditions they encounter will play a role in the years of their tenure. While God has shaped every aspect of a person's persona, it is their decision to choose the conditions and manner in which to fulfill the role they live by.

Every person is created equal, although no two people pose the exact same talents and /or skills, and no one person is more important or more significant than the next. Every skill and every talent is needed to interrelate with that of another, and others, in order to fulfill Gods plan for the world in which we live.

While it seems to be the nature of humanity to categorize and structure the status of people; in God's eyes, you, yes you, are just as important, significant, and necessary to the plan God has, for your life and the world as a whole. Just as it takes an undeterminable number of snowflakes of all shapes and sizes to make a snowman, only God knows and determines the number of people it takes to achieve His plan for the world. You, by the way, are one of them, a very important one in fact. Take pride in who you are and the gifts given you by God. Glorify God by applying those gifts by making the world a better place by your being a part of it.

TRADITION

Special holidays for many people are filled with tradition. Gatherings of family, friends, associates, and acquaintances with appropriate decorations, food, and beverages are frequently a significant part of the occasion. Good will, friendship, conversation, fun and games, all add pleasure, as well as warm feelings, to what many consider to be quality time spent with people who are significant to them and in their life. Sometimes, having been exposed to the traditions at a young age, through the years certain expectations remain as to how and what should happen on certain occasions.

Life has a way of changing expectations. What may have been a cohesive gathering of people such as family may no longer be possible or advantageous. As young people become adults and venture into the world, relationships, occupational opportunities, and just pure adventure itself pull them apart from earlier traditions. Soon they find that they are beginning new and perhaps far different traditions that are more suited with their new lifestyle and relationships. Seldom does a person lose the memories and warm feelings of those earlier traditions however. From time to time opportunities to be a part of a situation similar to one or more of those former traditional events may be possible and be fully appreciated.

There is one tradition that doesn't need a holiday for a reason to celebrate and be a part of. No need to acquire gifts, dress exquisitely, or even associate with others. This tradition doesn't have to wait for a specific date for it to be appropriate. In addition, you can remain at the event for whatever period of time you are comfortable, and no one will be offended if you leave only after a short period of time. The Host is the most accommodating, isn't argumentative or offensive, and gives you total and undivided attention. Best of all, if it's a tradition you've never been a part of, it can begin whenever you desire.

You've probably never considered establishing a tradition of spending time with God. Making it traditional to spend time with God in prayer and meditation will become one that will never be disappointing. One in which you will always come away with peaceful, fulfilling, and warm feelings. It need not be a special date on the calendar. Actually, any time spent with God in meditation and prayer is a special occasion, one that should be made traditional.

ABILITY TO GIVE

Most often we measure our ability to give in the form of materialistic ways when giving to the church, community organizations, political causes and candidates, even to our own families. Christmas, birthdays, anniversaries, and special occasions such as Valentine's Day, graduations, and even in memoriam of a deceased loved one or friend, are times when we are often made to feel compelled to give a material gift of money or some suitable material item, such as flowers or at least an appropriate card.

All these things are commendable and generally well received and sometimes even expected. There are times, however, when a person isn't in a position, whatever the reason, to give a material gift. Even though the emotional and heartfelt desire may be there, having fallen on hard times, being immobile, or otherwise lacking the means, one may not have the "Ability to Give". Sometimes, communicating with the other person, using a phone or some other electronic device, will fulfill that desire or the need, yet there may be circumstances where that is even unacceptable or impossible.

Yet the fact is however, regardless of circumstances, we all always have the "Ability to Give". The most precious and fulfilling and eternal gift is prayer! The perfect gift in all situations! God knows the true need one has at all times in every situation. One simple and meaningful prayer on the behalf of another can do more in the appropriate situation than any short-term satisfaction a material gift is able to provide.

A simple, heartfelt, and meaningful prayer may not get the "Oooos" and "Ahhhs" that a material gift will achieve. However, the satisfaction in knowing that you have blessed them with the hand of God being upon them will have a meaningful impact on their life. We never really know what is in another's heart, mind, or soul, what they are thinking, or what their attitude is in a particular situation, but God does. God knows better than they themselves know, what the true needs are they may have, particularly in fulfilling the plan God has for their life.

Prayer is the ultimate gift one is able to give under any circumstance or situation. The fact is, those blessings one prays over another will result in blessings in one's own life. While we may not always have the ability to shower material gifts on others, God has an abundant supply, desire, and ability to shower His blessings on all those who call upon Him. BE WARNED, this generous gift you give to others in the form of prayer may be reciprocated with huge unexpected blessings!

CHRISTMAS TREES

There are many people who look forward to the Christmas season and putting up and decorating a tree. Some who have bought artificial trees remove them from their storage containers, set them up, and proceed to decorate them with their favorite lights and ornaments. Others prefer the more traditional tree and venture to the nearby lot where trees are being sold.

There is also the opportunity in many areas where people are able to go to tree-growing farms, pick out their choice of tree, and cut it down themselves or have it cut down by an attendant. Yet there are those few who have the option of going to a wooded area where they are allowed to venture through in search for their ideal tree and cut it down. In either case it's a matter of securing it to their vehicle, bringing it home, to their office or business, setting it up, and getting it decorated.

Decorations are varied, be it the lights, ornaments, or other adornments, based on a person's preferences and ability and willingness to spend the money to acquire them. There are those who are very simple with inexpensive lights and ornaments, with some even taking the time to string popcorn and wrapping it around the tree. Others are extremely elaborate with themes, interactive lights, delicate or antique ornaments, and meticulously placed highlights, such as angel's hair, sparkling tinsel, and almost anything that one may delight in or imagine. Whatever the end result, the Christmas tree is generally a festive and joyful adornment for the holiday that pleases and lightens the spirit and contributes to a festive atmosphere.

Seldom does one consider the time, work, and care it took for them to be able to acquire a tree, real or fake, and all the trimmings. It takes several years after a seedling is placed in the ground, whether by hand or nature, along with much nourishment, water, and periodic trimming to produce that ideal specimen a person seeks to find.

Likewise, with artificial trees, those who produce them maintain equipment and employees who are dedicated to producing a life-like tree people are attracted to and purchase. The same is true with lights, ornaments, and other items made to enhance a tree.

Let us stop right there with the Christmas tree and give some thought to something few have ever likely considered. Have we ever looked at ourselves as being the tree and God being the one making it what it is when it is all decorated? Like the seedling contains every inherent feature providing the opportunity for it to grow into a beautiful evergreen, we are conceived with every human characteristic, including the Spirit of God within, to grow and develop into a glowing example of God's love and goodness. Like the evergreen, it takes time, proper care, and guidance for a person to fully develop into the person God called them to be and to be able to fulfill the plan God has for their life.

The decorations and other adornments? Those are the ways in which we are blessed by God. These blessings are the things that stand out and make us unique. Be it a personal attribute, skill, attitude, or even our demure, God uses these, in ways only He is able, to turn a person into a magnificent creature reflecting God's *love* and *goodness*. Isn't it amazing? Not only is God able to enhance our lives through His blessings, like the extremely elaborate Christmas tree, God is able to bring extremely elaborate experiences into our lives. The evergreen tree doesn't resist or hide, preventing a person from decorating it according to their plan and desires. We must not hide ourselves or resist God's plan for our lives.

In order to experience all of God's blessings and adornments in our lives, we must not only release ourselves to God's will for us, we must seek and implore God to intervene in our lives with the blessings that will be displayed and shine to glorify God. The Christmas tree and the manner in which it is decorated by a person reflects their willingness, resources, and dedication that maximizes the pleasure as to how it is viewed by others.

The way in which we live our lives displaying the blessings God has adorned our lives with, maximizing how we are viewed by others, displays the willingness, resources, and dedication of God's love for us and the way in which God is proactive in our lives.

Yes, just as a Christmas tree glitters, shines, and impresses, not because it is a simple evergreen, but because it has been adorned by someone, we also are able to glitter, shine, and impress, not because we are self-indulging, but because of the way in which God has adorned us with His blessings.

The Holy Spirit of God is with us;
we are blessed, guided, healed, protected,
prospered, whole, and strong. We have abun-
dance, well-being, and fulfillment. We are
instruments of God's love and peace and are
in God's safekeeping!

According to John 14:26, (paraphrased)
Jesus said, He (God) will give you another
Helper. . . **the Holy Spirit.**

IT'S AN A-MAZE-ING LIFE

Maze: a puzzle consisting of a network of paths and walls through which one has to find a way.

As a person faces a situation in life which they find challenging, yet a situation that must be experienced, as they step through the threshold of the situation they may only have a fuzzy idea, if any at all, as to how to get through it. All they can see is the pathway immediately before them. The path may appear to be very short, or extremely long. From their vantage point, perhaps all they can see is a path that may have many openings. One of those openings, which the person will likely choose to take, they hope will be the right one to get them through the situation in a way they determine will result in a satisfactory solution.

One can pursue the situation in a hit-or-miss way with anticipation that sooner or later they will take the openings and options along the path that will bring expedient results that resolve the situation. However, no matter which pathway one takes or which way they turn, there is no way to know which pathway will lead to the resolution, until they actually see the light at the end of the path. Until then, however, they may move along many paths, run into dead ends, retreat to where they entered that path, and find themselves having to select another pathway. Then only to repeat the process, time and time again, through trial and effort, to find the right path.

True, many of the paths taken may get a person closer to the path that leads to the final resolution of the situation. However, even then, can they be certain that this is the right resolution of the situation? Perhaps there are other paths that could be a means of exiting this maze in which one has found them self. A path may be chosen that appears to get through the situation; however, a path that merely leads to a new situation, also requiring to be passed through, only prolongs and worsens the situation. As long as the situation is continued to be pursued along a certain path, with no way of knowing where a path can be certain to lead, one may wonder aimlessly and never truly resolve the situation in such a way as to allow them to move on in life, leaving the situation behind as a non-issue.

A person may come across others in this maze and seek advice from them as to which pathway is the best and most expedient way out of the situation. Stopping and thinking about it, one will quickly realize that if the other person really knew which path was right for their situation, why are they in this maze? They are just as confused and lost. They are, at best, going by trial and error also. Yes, they may be able to advise that this or that path only leads to a dead-end. Yet you are both still standing here, neither having any idea which pathway is the best pathway to take to find the most direct way of resolving the situation.

Have no doubt that while a person may have no vision beyond the pathway they are on, God is looking down upon the situation and sees the entirety of the maze. God sees the most expedient and most favorable path to take to resolve the situation. God sees the paths that are only dead-ends, the paths that only lead back to where it all began, the long, long paths that end up leading nowhere. God also knows which exit from the maze leads to an unobstructed passageway to the future. God knows which exits only lead to another and yet another maze just prolonging and complicating the situation.

Yet, how many times in life do we indignantly, bull-headedly strike out on our own, simply ignoring the fact that only God knows the most direct and expedient way in life to follow to resolve every situation? No matter how seemingly insignificant, difficult, or threatening one may imagine a situation may be, God is there to direct us through the maze. The fact is, as one wonders aimlessly through the maze, God's desire is to reach out and provide the direction needed. First however, we must be willing to "Let Go — Let God" and release the situation to God. We must admit that without God's divine guidance we will only aimlessly wonder endlessly.

THE EAGLE SOARS

Just as the thermal enables the eagle to soar to incredible heights,
so also, the grace of God enables us to sour to supernatural heights.

An incredible experience and lesson today, the 11th of April 2010 about 1:30 p.m.

I had just finished my Sunday brunch, having enjoyed it outside because of what a beautiful day it was, on the little patio by my garden house. I was surveying the tree line along the easterly lot line of the property as I contemplated some things I wanted to do to improve it by removing a couple of trees that were crowding out others and not allowing them to fill out nicely. Looking up at the trees, a bird caught my eye as it flew just into my view. It was very low, maybe a hundred feet above the tallest tree. Its markings with a brilliant white neck, head, and fanning tail unmistakenly distinguished it as an eagle. Eagles are rare in this area of southwestern Michigan. However, it has been documented that there are some eagles that spend the summer a few miles north of the city on a small island in the middle of a wide section of a river, which flows through the area.

As I watched the eagle, it began to circle above me. Obviously having caught a thermal, the eagle circled around and around, soaring higher and higher. I don't recall seeing the bird flap its wings even once after I started observing it. Right above me in clear sight the eagle soared higher and higher.

The day was beautiful and the temperature near the ground was in the high 50s, perhaps 57 ° or 58°. There were very few clouds and they were very high in the sky. The eagle soared higher and higher in a very deliberate circle above me, always in my direct line of vision. I had to hold my hands to my face to shield the direct sunlight from obscuring my vision.

I continued to watch for perhaps ten minutes, maybe more, as with a wondrous sight like this one tends to lose all track of time. The eagle soared closer and closer to the clouds, then began to soar through the thinner clouds and ultimately soared into and out of the denser clouds. It did this effortlessly while never doing anything more than directing the pitch of its wings to enable it to circle and climb higher. As the eagle became almost lost in the clouds, it ceased circling and soared off to the north, presumably off to its nesting place north of town.

This incredible sight was not only awesome to watch, but an affirmation from God about the events in my life at this very time. You see, for some time, I have been spiritually inspired through my daily meditation to stop flapping my wings and trying to make things happen.

I daily thank God for inspiring me to plow the right fields and scatter the proper seeds and then release it to His hand to allow Him to provide the water and sunshine to make it grow. In other words, doing the things that are humanly required, necessary, which I am able to do in a given situation, and then letting go and letting God do the supernatural. For some time now, even before this viewing of the eagle, I had compared my situation to that of the eagle. While the eagle must, with its powerful wings, fly to the level to catch the thermal, it instinctively knows to stop flapping its wings and ride the thermal. Likewise, with God, it is important to do what I can do in a situation. Then it's equally important to know when to stop trying to force the issue and rely on the grace of God to enable me to soar to supernatural heights.

Today's presence of that eagle, directly over my head, precisely when I was outside looking up at the treetops, was no chance thing. It was so obvious, so deliberate, so complete an example that I believe it to be an affirmation by God. A lesson, an example that just as the thermal enables the eagle to soar to incredible heights, so also the grace of God enables us to soar to supernatural heights! Therefore, do what you can, but don't force an issue. That only delays God from being able to raise you to the incredible heights, He desires for you to be uplifted to, also through His graces. God taught through Jesus Christ and the parables he spoke when He walked upon this earth, and God continues to do this today by showing us the way.

If we hear Him when He communicates with us, if we listen to Him, if we try to understand what He is telling us, and if we make every effort to follow His guidance, we have no need to flap our wings unnecessarily attempting to make things happen. God will enable us to soar to supernatural heights!

Allow the radiant light of newness to

illuminate your way

as you move forward

FINAL THOUGHT

At some point a person may look at their life and all the things that are happening in their life and conclude; "You know, the world and everything that I am a part of would go on if I ceased to be involved with it. Absolutely nothing would come to a halt. No one really needs me or the contributions I make in the things I'm involved with".

Then again, they may reconsider and think; I still possess many talents, skills, and abilities. All the characteristics that aided me throughout my life and contributed to the many achievements and accomplishments are still a part of me. Perhaps some have become dulled or tarnished, and it may take longer to complete certain tasks. On the other hand, there are personal traits that are continuing to become stronger and improve.

No matter one's age or position in life, as long as a person is alive and breathing, God has a plan for their life. No matter their state of health, physical ability, mental capacity, or state of mind, God has a way to use the gifts they are blessed with to fulfill His plan for their life. Even if it is the inspiration that others may experience through the mutual contact or the awareness of particular circumstances.

It is said that Jesus Christ was about thirty years of age before He started His ministry. In three short years His impact on people through His teachings of love and peace was not only an inspiration for those to whom He ministered at the time, but it has endured for centuries. Jesus released Himself to God, and God, through Jesus, demonstrated to mankind His love, compassion, healing, and restoration to make people whole and strong and by setting aside the things of the past and by being forgiving.

God also works through ordinary people to do extraordinary things. When a person releases themselves to God, a ministry begins to evolve through them where God uses their talents to fulfill His plan. Perhaps no one really needs you or the contributions you make in the things that you're involved with. However, those many talents, skills, and abilities you still possess will be used by God.

It's not that a person should discontinue their normal routine of life. God is able to utilize one's ministry in their everyday life. As the person interacts with their family, friends, and even strangers, wherever they may go or whatever they may be involved in, God will use them to be a blessing through their ministry.

For those who have read what has been presented here and may have lost that igniter and spark, I beseech God to use one word, phrase, sentence, paragraph, or analogy from these writings to ignite that flame and "Awaken the Power of the Spirit Within". May they release themselves to God's plan for their life and begin their ministry.

My ministry is to
"Awaken the Power of the Spirit Within"
and ignite that flame.

Jesus said;
I do not speak on my own authority, but the Father who dwells in me.
John 14:10—16 (ESV)

Has your ministry begun?

ABOUT THE AUTHOR

Patrick has lived a full life. At the age of seventy-nine, his life experiences are varied and colorful, sometimes dark and gray, while other times full of light in an array of beautiful colors.

Raised on a rural farm in the central part of a midwestern state, the author, having a lack of peers to associate with in his younger years, spent many hours of imaginary playtime. Then, attending a parochial school in the big city some distance from his home for twelve years, often being considered an outsider, life experiences could be somewhat challenging at times. In his teens and early adulthood, an appreciation for music and the recognition of his musical talent became a springboard for personal growth and confidence in public venues. While considered to be a mere average student in school, his creativity, a likely result of his childhood imagination, proved to be an asset in later life as he developed in-depth procedural outlines from sales and marketing tools to entrepreneurial business development and operational plans.

A keen interest in craftsmanship in the use wood, as well as his fundamental concept of seeing things as they could be rather than as they are, peaked his interest in restoration and involvement in construction. This same restoration mindset became the driving force in the author's desire to awaken the recognition of God's role in people's lives.

Just as the author himself turned away from recognizing how God had been proactive in his life, in retrospect he came to realize the many ways in which he has been blessed. While his belief may have been strong, he came to accept that at the very best, he took God for granted.

Developing a personal relationship with God, realizing God is a true forever friend, companion, confidant, is surely an amazing experience — one that a person is all too often denied because of earlier experiences in life that have caused one to become disenchanted with the things of spirituality. Seeing things as they could be, as in one's relationship with God, rather than as they are, is the author's intent in his commitment in sharing the written word.

ACKNOWLEDGMENTS

While there are many individuals who have been an influential part of my life, thereby having a significant role contributing to the events and circumstances presented here, family and friends have certainly been the most dominating. My mother Laline, was certainly supportive and encouraging in childhood years. Father Leo exemplified dedication and hard work. Brother James and Sister Dorothy, both much older in age than I, weaved paths challenging to follow. Fatherly experiences throughout the spontaneity in the lives of sons Michael and Daniel and daughter Sherri evoke the blessings by which their individuality added love, joy and pride in my life. Granddaughters Reagan and Allison exemplify Michael's and Sherri's dedication to parenthood by providing sound foundations for growth and development to adulthood.

Throughout adolescent and teen years, positive as well as in some cases negative circumstances, influenced significant behavioral patterns in my life. However, the skill and enthusiasm of a Football Coach in seventh and eighth grade developed self-confidence, and a positive conviction of self-determination and ability which I had previously lacked. Likewise, Ursula Klein, the High School music teacher and my personal voice coach contributed immensely in the development of my talents, skills and personality traits.

Occupationally, a Chief of Police in the small town in which I was an officer for a few years, then the manager and assistant manager of the Insurance agency where my career flourished, and others were all uplifting and supportive in enriching the experiences in my life.

While some experience friendships which remain steadfast in a person's life, few in my life have persisted, be it in their having passed as in the case of Bill Fox and John Cavaluchi, or simply in the case of life changing circumstances. Yet imbedded in this text, are encounters of friendship, be it a companionship or simply with a passing stranger.

Many unlikely sources are contributable to the Inspirational and Spiritual foundation underlying the development of ideas and philosophical contributions I have put forth. While having read the Bible in its entirety has certainly played a role, the continual awareness of the Holy Spirit of God, while not physically seen, not recognizably heard, not grasped by touch, and with my cries perhaps not having been heard aloud, the gentle piece of the Holy Spirit within has prevailed in providing the inspiration to persist in bringing forth what has been presented here.

Pertaining to the production of this publication, the encouragement, time in reviewing text, and prayerful support of good friend Katie Wood is unmeasurable in my degree of appreciation. Through the cooperative efforts of the staff of Mill City Press, what has been brought into reality here, may be an opportunity to Awaken in the lives of readers a renewed relationship with God.

CPSIA information can be obtained
at www.ICGtesting.com
Printed in the USA
BVHW04s2344220918
528137BV00009B/314/P

9 781545 638149